Goin' Dialin'

Stories from Ossabaw and Sapelo Islands
(and a few tug boating stories)

By: Mike Sellers

[signature: Mike Sellers]

Copyright 2017
Michael Sellers, all rights reserved

Goin' Dialin'

My good friend Noel Holcomb told me this story about running into Ossabaw's Island Manager, Roger, at the mainland dock one day. Roger asked him, "You goin' dialin'?" Noel said," Excuse me?" Roger repeated the question, Noel was perplexed. He finally figured out that Roger was asking," Are you going to the island?"

A mixture of Geechee, redneck Bryan County Georgia and English was the language Roger was speaking. Once Noel recognized the language barrier, he got better at communicating with Roger. It took a while.

But when I thought back on that, I figured, "What better name for my book?"

It has Geechee, redneck, and just southern charm all rolled into one.

Goin' Dialin'

Introduction

Ossabaw and Sapelo Islands are remote islands off the Georgia coast. Both are mostly state owned and neither have bridges connecting them to the mainland. As my friend, supervisor, shooting instructor and mentor Noel, used to always say, "An island is a body of land surrounded by the necessity of a boat."

Well said. So, living on these islands always centered around having boats, running boats, maintaining boats and cussing boats when they didn't act right. Like the 18 foot Galaxy we had on Ossabaw, it had a bad habit of dying when you got right up to the floating dock. Crash! It always started and ran fine, up until that very moment when you shifted to reverse. Boats don't have brake pedals, you shift to reverse to stop your forward motion.

Anyway, I used to sit around with fellow employees and friends and tell these stories, about boats, explosions, shark fishing, tug boating, etc. A few years ago, I wrote a story called "How to Hunt With the Game Warden" and posted it on Facebook. Lots of friends commented on the story so I wrote more and posted them. Soon everyone was telling me that I needed to write these stories down and publish them in a book.

Well here it is, such as it is. I hope you enjoy it.

The Beginning

My brother Joe and his wife Sharen moved to Sapelo Island, Georgia in November of 1976, on Election Day. Jimmy Carter was elected president that day. Jimmy used to visit Sapelo often when he was governor of Georgia. This whole move came about because Sharen's uncle was a TV repairman for Sears.

I got introduced to loading a barge that day. I thought it was really cool, but slightly dangerous having all of my brother's belongings precariously teetering on oak planks over the water. Little did I know that Sapelo politics were involved. We were told to load at one location, then told to go several miles to another location to load. This was at the time of changes to the operation of the island. The Department of Natural Resources (DNR) and the University of Georgia Marine Institute (UGAMI) were now having to cooperate.

The largest roadblock to this cooperation was the fact that these people hated each other's guts!

I made a habit out of visiting Joe and Sharen on Sapelo. I was amazed at the opportunity that some people got to live and work in such a beautiful environment. Joe had told me about positions available in the DNR, such as Wildlife Technician positions. He arranged for me to meet with the regional supervisor, C.V. to discuss careers in DNR. I was told that the state was purchasing Ossabaw Island from Mrs. West and family and that

Goin' Dialin'

there was a very good chance that they would need a mechanic on the island since they ran generators for electricity, twenty-four hours a day. There was a lot of competition for wildlife jobs, not so much for mechanic jobs. I was enrolled at Brunswick College at the time, in the Automotive Repair class under the instruction of Colin White, a great teacher and a great guy.

As luck would have it, or providence, or whatever, a fire broke out while I was on the island that weekend. The pump on the fire truck would not start. This fine piece of equipment was a nineteen fifty something Georgia Forestry surplus truck equipped with a gasoline powered pump. I diagnosed the problem as a defective fuel pump. They replaced the fuel pump a few days later, and the engine ran fine, sometimes I'm lucky! I'd much rather be lucky than good, is my motto. We worked hard putting out the fire with "fire flaps", a fire flap is something like a mud flap on a pole. The regional supervisor, C.V., was impressed with my work ethic and with the fact that I had correctly diagnosed the fuel pump as the culprit.

While I'm on the subject of work ethic, something greatly missing in the current generation, I got mine from working with my Aunt Bonnie and Uncle Spencer when I was a teenager. Uncle Spencer owned a feed and seed store in Brunswick Georgia, where I grew up. I would work there during the "busy season", which was spring time. People would plant gardens and need seed, fertilizer and plants to get them going. It was wall to wall packed with people in the feed store during busy season. The first year I worked there, I stopped, had to have a break! I went to the soda machine and got an ice-cold Dr. Pepper from the machine that you put change in, then pull the soda out of the row. I kicked back and was enjoying my Dr. Pepper, when I heard my Aunt Bonnie say, "Mike, if you're Uncle Spencer sees you taking a soda break while this place is full of customers, he will fire you!" I sat my Dr. Pepper down (to warm) and got back to work waiting on customers. I never again "took a break" during busy season.

Guitars…Cadillac's…Hillbilly Music…

Mr. White, my Automotive Repair instructor at Brunswick College, asked me once if I played a guitar, I told him yes, I'd been playing since I was seven or eight years old. He told me to bring my guitar to his house one evening because, and I quote," You will starve to death as a mechanic, I need to teach you some way to make a living."
I went to Mr. White's house; he was one heck of a guitar player! He taught me his method of thumb picking and strumming, he was a great teacher. My rendition of "Wildwood Flower" was because of his instruction.
Guitar picking became an important pastime on the remote islands I have lived on.

It helps to be able to make your own entertainment when you live in a remote place. I picked with and learned things from several friends over the years. In later years my son, Ike, and I sat around many evenings picking guitars and making up songs instead of hovering in front of a television.

Ossabaw

I have been blessed to have the privilege of living in two of the most beautiful places that God created.

The State of Georgia bought Ossabaw Island in 1978. Joe let me know that they were looking for a mechanic on Ossabaw and introduced me to the wildlife biologist there named Jerry McCollum, whom became known as "Big Mac". Jerry interviewed me for the job on Ossabaw and I got it. Well, he sort of interviewed me, we had an informal discussion about life on a remote island and if I thought I could live with that.

My new wife, Lisa, and I moved to Ossabaw Island on December 28, 1978. DNR had built three new houses on Ossabaw, at Bahia grass field, on Cain Patch Creek, we lived in the first one you came to when headed south. Number One, Pine Barrens Road was our address. The night we moved there, they were having a Christmas party at the Main House, we attended and got to meet the folks there.

Goin' Dialin'

That night we met the island boat captain Stanfield and his wife Mary. We also met his brother Roger, who was the island manager and his wife Sarah. Four people that we would really get to know and love in years to come. We also met Mrs. West, who sold the island to the state, against her nieces and nephews will. A character, well, all we met were characters! I later came to believe that you don't HAVE to be crazy to live on a remote island, but it helps. Mrs. West's housekeeper, Queenie Mae Williams was introduced to me and just gave me the biggest hug, she was a sweet lady.

Mrs. West sold the island to the state and retained a life estate. She owns the mansion and 20 or 30 acres until she dies. When we moved there, she was in her seventies. I had been told that she wouldn't live much longer, as one state official put it, she had been," Rode hard and put up wet."

As of this writing, April 2018, Mrs. West just turned 105 years old. She has outlived most of the state officials that were involved with the sale. The ones that are still alive have long since retired.

Goin' Dialin'

DNR

When I moved to Ossabaw, we had a brand-new shop, a Craftsman tool box full of wrenches, sockets and screwdrivers. We had a new drill press and a table saw that Donnie Fears and I had to take out of the box and assemble. We also had an air compressor. That was pretty much it.

Now any mechanic worth his salt knows that you need a lot more stuff to operate a decent shop. We had purchasing regulations within the state and even more within our region of Game Management. The state had a rule that anything costing over one hundred dollars had to have three bids before purchasing, our regional rule reduced that to twenty-five dollars.

We needed things, like a welder, a tire changer, those are kind of big-ticket items that should require bids, but we needed other, small things. Things like a tire gauge, needle valve tool, etc. These things cost a couple of bucks each but there were so many! I started making lists, I went to an auto parts store and when the total got up to twenty-four dollars and some odd cents, I would have to stop and go to another auto parts store. Mind you, this was before the days of purchasing cards, which the state came up with many years later, we had to open an account at all these places, we would then be billed at the end of the month, and if the total spent in a particular month came to more than, yep you guessed it, twenty-five dollars, I was ordered to complete a telephone bid sheet to accompany the bill.

Goin' Dialin'

Okay, I was wising up here. I started writing up my lists in triplicate, go to Savannah, drop off my lists to three different vendors and come back later, pick up the bids, go to the lowest one and make my purchase. When friends and family came to visit, I particularly remember when Mark Hanson came over, I showed him my tire valve tool. "This little jewel had three bids, one dollar and seventy-eight cents. Glad we saved the state of Georgia on that one, could have been a dollar seventy-nine!"

Of course, my time and gasoline to go to all these places were never considered in this insanity. This is where I learned another lesson, go with the flow, don't bring logic and reason into the state's inner workings. It has no business there.

Brownlee

Ol' Brownlee was a trip. Brownlee worked for Mrs. West on Ossabaw. He was Queenie Mae Williams lifetime partner and a great guy. Brown was a one-legged black man, a small fellow, very meek. Roger could always tell when Brown was raiding his garden because Brown had a peg leg. When you leave one footprint and a round indention in the soil, it's pretty obvious.

Goin' Dialin'

I had conversations with Brown often. I asked him once how he lost his leg. He explained that he was in a bar in Savannah when he got caught in a crossfire. He took a bullet in the leg and had to have it amputated.

Brown approached me one day at the DNR shop.

"Any wimmins round here?"

I looked up and down Main Road and replied," Don't see any." I had no idea where this conversation was going.

Brown pulled a new peg leg from behind the seat of his truck, Richard Bowen had made it I found out later. Brown quickly dropped his pants, "I need you to make me a bracket to attach this new leg to my nub of a leg."

Well, what you going to do after such a request?

I went and got a tape measure, measured all the crucial measurements, and told Brown to come back in a few days. I do remember looking up and down the road; we were still outside of the shop and hoping that no one came by while I was prodding Brown with the tape measure, with his pants down! Could be embarrassing!

I made the bracket for Brown's peg leg, attached the wooden leg to the bracket and that was that. About a month later, I asked Brown why I hadn't seen him wearing his new leg.

He said," That laig is too good to wear around here; I only wear that laig to church on Sunday."

Ol' Brownlee died while I was on Ossabaw, at his funeral, I discovered that his name was James Brownlee. I never knew anything but Brownlee or Brown.

A one-legged blackbird hung around Torrey Landing for months after Brown's death. Hum?

Queenie Mae

Queenie Mae Williams worked for Mrs. West doing cooking, cleaning and whatever. We named our work boat after Queenie. This was McCollum's idea. He and I stopped at Queenie and Brown's house one day. We were talking to them, they broke out a bag of pork rinds, and Big Mac and I were scarfing them down. Big Mac dropped one on the floor, picked it up and ate it. Later, I mentioned to Big Mac that I was always taught to trash chips dropped on the floor. His answer," I would not insult Queenie Mae that her floor wasn't clean enough to eat off." Smart Big Mac was.

I've had three really great bosses since I've been in the working world. Big Mac was my first, gave me latitude to do what I wanted while maintaining an overall control. A good boss recognizes employees' abilities and gives the employee latitude to do his or her job as he or

Goin' Dialin'

she sees fit. A good boss will also chew your sorry tail out if you mess up.

When I moved to Sapelo in April of 1985, I noticed that there were lots of hard feelings between DNR and the University of Georgia Marine Institute (UGAMI). The UGAMI had been running things for quite a number of years, had support from R.J. Reynolds money that came through the Sapelo Foundation. They also got tons of grants from the National Science Foundation and others, so they were well funded at the time. They had over eight scientists that did full time research on Sapelo and published papers, which was a big money maker for the Institute.

My boss, Bob, called me to the carpet one day, this was years later when I was running the ferry to Sapelo. I had arranged with another employee to have a cookout at his house. I thought he was going to pick up the ribs and when he returned to the boat, he didn't have them. My friend Raj, and I jumped into the DNR truck and took off for the grocery store! This was back when the last run was at 5:15 PM. We had less than 15 minutes to get ribs, the grocery store was eight miles away, get back to the boat and run on time.

Well, we were a little late leaving that day. When Bob called me down on this escapade, I replied that we were trying to get the DNR and University folks together, "Think of the big picture." We are trying to get these two state entities together, parties, poker games, etc. were intended to get folks talking and involved with one another and relieve some of the animosity between the two.

I also prompted all the cute young female research technicians at the party to tell Bob, how this is so nice to promote the camaraderie between DNR and the UGAMI. Bob still chewed me out on this, as he was eating the ribs that I purchased earlier.

The next day, after he called me to the carpet, he said," You know that the worst thing that you did was drive a state truck to the grocery store."

I replied, "We had to drive a state truck, we would have gotten a speeding ticket if we had driven a personal vehicle!"

I think Bob appreciated my honesty, I'm not sure.

Back to Ossabaw

Billy, Al and Jim Bo

Now, don't go writing any letters, I know how racist the name Jim Bo sounds, but it was his name. Jim Bo was Billy and Al's father. Billy, Al and Jim Bo lived at the first cabin you saw when headed south on Ossabaw. The cabins were tabby cottages, made for slaves in the plantation era. They were remodeled and really good

Goin' Dialin'

houses. Stanfield and Mary lived in the second one, Queenie and Brownlee lived in the third house.

Jim Bo, Billy and Al were employed by Mrs. West on Ossabaw Island. They did landscaping and whatever. They were also avid fishermen and hunters. They supplemented their income with selling fish and raccoons to "city folks" in Savannah.

Our regional supervisor made the mistake of confronting Mrs. West with the small legal technicality of selling wildlife. I think she put him on the straight and narrow pretty quickly!

Roger would always tell me that Billy and Al would not tell him where they caught fish. I, on the other hand, would exchange fishing information with Billy and Al and they, as far as I know, never lied to me about location, tide, etc. It's all about trust folks.

My Dad loved to troll for seatrout in the fall and winter, if another boat approached, he would hold his pole over the side of the boat, he did not want anyone to see him catch a fish! I inquired if he thought someone would come and catch all the fish, he explained no, he had his favorite spots and every sumadagun and his brother would be in them if he was seen catching fish.

Roger

Roger was a cowboy, a Georgia cowboy. Roger loved cattle, had a bunch of them on Ossabaw. Roger was Mrs. West's island manager and owned all the cattle on the island. His limit, according to the DNR, was 200, he always swore that was all of them. We decided that it was more like 400. But Roger would always give us a cow to feed out and butcher, he would never take money. We usually bought him a new gun and forced him to take it. He and his wife Sarah would help us butcher the beef and cut and wrap it. It was a great deal!

Boats, Dreaming of Boats and More Ossabaw Stories

I love boats, well, actually, I hate boats. Okay, I love boats, but boating may be the problem. Maybe I ran boats too long. I love workboats, tugs, ferries, barges, scows and other non-descript craft, as the Coast Guard rules call them.

Maybe I should tell you how this all came about; I realize that it's not making much sense. My sister-in-law's uncle was a TV repairman for Sears. Glad I cleared that up. Back to boating.

I remember gazing at a Detroit Diesel brochure about work boats in the 1980's. It had tug boats in there that I drooled over. They were beautiful. I fell head over heels in love with the lines, the power, ah, the raw

Goin' Dialin'

power! My eyes would glaze over; I would be headed all over the world, pushing barges, making the world work. I was living and working on Ossabaw Island, Georgia at the time as a mechanic for the Georgia Department of Natural Resources, the most hated agency in the state of Georgia I always called it.

I worked for DNR for twenty-five years and took an early retirement at age forty-five with over twenty-five years of service. I pretty much had to retire or kill somebody. It was a toss-up. Let's just say that me and bureaucracy don't mix. I did the bureaucracy thing for twenty-five years, fill out the proper forms, make sure everything is nice and neat and within the specifications, and zoom! Through the halls of Wisdom, Justice, and Moderation, the machine would perform as designed and produce results, sometimes. Big Mac, my first boss with DNR compared state paperwork to a dollar changing machine, "Get all the wrinkles out, fold down those corners, put in the proper orientation, and BINGO! Change appears!"

I was a good employee. I always sent in the proper paperwork, got my telephone bids in order and did as I was told. I never had a supervisor who wasn't thrilled with my job performance and skills.

Goin' Dialin'

Lisa and I Have a Big Announcement

We both looked down into the vial. A circle was on the bottom. We then looked at the instructions of the home pregnancy test. A circle on the bottom meant she was definitely "with child" as they used to say. It was early summer 1979. Our son Ike was being magically created in the womb of his mother. In later years, we would always say, "I remember when he was just a little circle."

But we had to break this news to our co-workers and other island residents, we were sort of worried because one reason we were hired was that we had no children. When you live on a remote island, there is the slight problem of school. There was no everyday ferry and definitely no school on the island.

After we broke the news to Big Mac, he said," I can't think of a better place to raise a child." We felt better.

Noel immediately wanted to teach him how to hunt and fish, he was elated.

"What about school?" I asked.

"That's at least five years down the road, let's not worry about that, we'll figure it out," was their reply.

Goin' Dialin'

Some of Noel's Teaching

When Ike was about two years old, Noel killed (or allegedly killed) a rattlesnake. He decided to bring it to our house and show Ike what a rattlesnake looked like and make sure that Ike didn't play with these critters and give them plenty of room. A pretty good lesson in dealing with the natural world that was Ossabaw.

Oops! We went out to where Noel had dumped the snake in our front yard. No snake. Lisa immediately started calling him a liar. I started looking for a snake. Noel joined me, we finally found the snake about seventy-five feet from where Noel had dumped him.

Valuable lesson for Ike and Noel. Ike, look out for rattlesnakes. Noel, don't piss off Mama!

The Tree

I worked for Noel Holcomb on Ossabaw. Noel is the only person that I know that started out as a Wildlife Technician I and moved up to eventually be Commissioner of the Department of Natural Resources, an amazing man, a great friend and mentor. Noel and I were cutting "beetle trees" (pine trees which were infected and killed by the Southern Pine Beetle) on the south end of Ossabaw along with Tony Tucker, our safety man. The plan was to cut the trees into a pile and spray the pile with insecticide to kill the beetles. Noel had cut a pine tree which fell wrong and hung up in a live oak tree. He decided to cut the oak to get the pine to the ground where we could spray it. It looked to me and all of us that the trees were going to fall away from me. I was cutting another tree into the pile; I had to turn my back on Noel for just a short time to notch the pine tree that I was cutting. I remember Tony yelling, "WATCH OUT!" as a 10-inch diameter live oak limb hit me across my back. The pine leaning against it had pivoted the live oak and sent it in my direction. I have never been hit so hard, I remember being pushed into the dirt, and thinking," That sure wasn't much warning!"

I was hurt! Bad! Noel just knew I was dead. He told me later that he didn't even want to go look, because he just knew that I was dead. I was writhing on the ground with the breath knocked out of me, begged him to hit me on the back so I could get a breath. He said," No way am I hitting you on the back, you may have spinal injuries." Noel was always cool in a crisis. I managed to finally get my breathing back to normal. Then came the painful ten-mile trip to the north end on bumpy dirt roads, I was close to passing out from pain by the time we got there. Then an eight-mile boat ride to the mainland, and finally we arrived at St. Joseph's Hospital in Savannah. They x-rayed me twice; the doctors could not believe nothing was broken. My back was one solid bruise!

Now, for those of you who don't believe in God, I feel sorry for you. (I personally don't believe in atheists!) Six inches higher, the ten-inch limb would have hit me in the head and I would not be sitting here writing this story.

Ike would have never known his dad. Lisa was pregnant with our son Ike at the time. If the limb hadn't knocked me clear, I would have been smashed like a bug under that tree. I think the good Lord had looked down and thought," That ol' boy, I know he was baptized when he was fourteen years old, but I want to give him something to think about for the rest of his life, and I'm not through with him yet." I have thought about that day, often. (I always picture God as having a southern accent!)

HURRICANE DAVID

A month after the "tree incident", we had to evacuate for hurricane David. Big Mac was on vacation in Wyoming. It was Labor Day, 1979. We had loaded up the thirty-two-foot workboat, "Queenie Mae Williams" for evacuation; we looked like refugees from some third world country! All we needed was a goat to really complete the picture. We had dogs, cats and everybody with all their precious possessions piled on the boat. Well Noel got underway with the Queenie Mae, left me to bring Big Mac's seventeen-foot Boston Whaler. Shortly after Noel got underway he had problems. The boat builders for some insane reason had used PVC pipe on the cooling system, which was a keel cooler. A keel cooler is a set of bronze pipes that run along the bottom of the boat which engine cooling water runs through; the other option is a heat exchanger, which would pump seawater through a chamber of bronze pipes. Anyway, the PVC fell apart and the engine started to overheat.

Goin' Dialin'

We were approaching the Swash, which was a narrow channel between Ossabaw and Green Island sounds, we got a line to the Queenie Mae and secured it to the bow of the Whaler. I pulled hard on the line, in reverse and got the boat back into the channel. Once in the creek, we re-rigged and got the Queenie Mae into a stern tow. It was a long trip, from the Swash to Vernon View, towing a 32-foot displacement hull boat with a 17-foot Boston Whaler with a seventy-horsepower outboard motor!

Our hurricane plan consisted of us, after unloading passengers at Vernon View, running the Queenie Mae up the Ogeechee River and riding out the storm. We were young and dumb at the time. Boy, were we young and dumb at the time.

Noel and I tied the disabled Queenie Mae up, as best we could, between the Vernon View dock and the neighbor's dock. She survived the storm, was still there and still disabled when we returned.

We pulled Big Mac's boat out, put it on the trailer, and headed to Big Mac's wife's apartment in Savannah. Lisa headed to Brunswick to her Mom's.

Hurricane David was a category one storm with ninety mile-per-hour winds. The destruction from this storm gave me a new respect for hurricanes. I can't imagine a category two, three, four or five! When we left the apartment after the storm, we came to a distinct line of where the eye of the storm had come through. There were trees and power poles, power lines, down exactly in the path of this storm. You could actually see where the eye of the storm came through Savannah.

When we returned to the Island, there were downed trees everywhere, huge old live oaks down on every road. Noel and I were clearing one of the most used roads; he cut a large limb, and guess where it fell. Yep, right on yours truly! "Dang Noel, I thought the first one was an accident, but now I'm beginning to wonder!" From that day forward, if Noel picked up a chainsaw, I headed in the other direction.

Hogs

Noel and I were riding around one day, got to Willows Road and there was this big boar hog at the intersection of Main Road and Willows. Noel jumped out, shot the hog, and we went over to inspect. The hog was in his death throes, it was cold, and steam was coming out of every breath. Noel asked," Where did I hit him?" I said," From the steam, I think you hit him in the radiator!" That story went viral, well viral for the eighties, which was word of mouth. Everybody knew that story and laughed about it.

Hogs were a nuisance on Ossabaw, raccoons would predate a sea turtle nest, leave some eggs, hogs would eat the entire nest and look for more. I guess that's why they call them hogs.

During turtle nesting season, we would shoot hogs all night and reload bullets in the daytime. I was reloading 30-30 bullets one day when Noel came to me and said that the regional office got a complaint that we were," Shooting hogs and letting them lay." The complaint came from useless poachers who were making money catching Ossabaw hogs and selling hunts for "Russian Wild Boar." Our regional supervisor asked Noel how many hogs we had killed and "let lay." Noel told him about 30 hogs. When alone, we laughed and spontaneously said, "About 300!" Again, animal lovers, they were extremely detrimental to loggerhead sea turtle nests. I have no regrets. What would you rather have, feral hogs or sea turtles?

Donkeys

Ossabaw was rich with wildlife, with a few surprises. Mrs. West, a wonderful and kind lady, had owned Ossabaw for many years before selling it, at a great discount, to the State of Georgia. If she hadn't loved the island so much, and been the "eccentric" lady that she was, she would have sold it to developers and it would be another "Hilton Head". It is a wonderful Heritage Preserve today because of this gracious lady.

Sometime back in the late 1960's or early 1970's Mrs. West and her husband, heard about these Sicilian donkeys on Bull Island South Carolina that were going to be destroyed because they were overpopulating the

Goin' Dialin'

island. They rescued four of these donkeys and carried them to Ossabaw. Well duh, they started overpopulating Ossabaw in a few years!

One little known fact about donkeys, they have the libido of about six eighteen-year-old male humans combined! They are constantly "doing it". Almost always, if we were doing a tour of VIP's somewhere along the way there would be donkeys in the throes of love.
When the state bought Ossabaw, they said that something had to be done about the donkeys. Mrs. West agreed to have the male donkeys castrated.
Enter Penn State University. Someone at Penn State wanted to study the habits of feral donkeys. Since castration would affect the normal behavior of the donkeys, they proposed, and it was accepted, that the male donkeys would be given vasectomies. All the donkeys were inventoried and tagged. The males were given vasectomies. Well, some of those vasectomies apparently didn't take, or maybe they missed one or two. Baby donkeys started showing up a few years later.

I'll never forget the Penn State crew following donkeys around with funnels and bottles attached to long poles to collect donkey urine, what a sight! What a job.
" So, what do you do for a living?"
"I catch donkey urine with a funnel and a jar."
Something to add to your resume' right there!

Goin' Dialin'

Eleanor T. West

Mrs. West, best known as Sandy, was a great animal lover who rescued donkeys, continually fought the DNR about eradicating the feral hog population, and generally didn't like hunting. Her father, Dr. Tory, was an avid hunter and had enjoyed African safaris and accumulated many hunting trophies in his lifetime which are still displayed at her home on Ossabaw. He also left her many millions of dollars in inheritance. Because of which she never had to work a day in her life. She did work at what she loves, which is art, and supported I don't know how many artists through the Ossabaw Foundation. She is a wonderful lady, and I love her dearly.

She sold the island to the State of Georgia in 1978; Governor George Busbee was the key on making this deal happen. This deal came with a life estate for Sandy, as long as she lives, she can stay on the island and owns the mansion and 30 acres. She was about 70 years old at the time of the deal. I've heard it said that she," Would not live very much longer." She is now over a hundred years old, has outlived Governor Busbee and all the DNR officials involved have since retired or died. She was always nice to my family and me when we lived there and even after we left. She babysat our son, Ike, several times when he was a baby (he would not accept cookies from her because of the dead roaches in the cookie jar, she did not believe in exterminators).

Goin' Dialin'

She did not believe in killing mice either, her son Justin, with help from the maintenance staff, built a live trap for mice. They would fall into it and be cushioned from the fall by foam rubber (to keep from giving them concussions or brain damage). Roger Parker once asked Justin where he was going, Justin told him that he was going to the south end of the island to release captured mice. Roger said," You are driving to the south end to release a mouse?" Justin's reply was no, not one mouse, I'm taking two!

I was reminded several times while I lived on Ossabaw that if Mrs. West hadn't been so "eccentric", we would not have been there. She would have sold out to developers and the Island would not be the wonderful, protected place that it is today. I've had to remind island managers that came after us of that fact.

When the contractors finished the DNR shop, they stained the wood siding with a stain that came out yellowish. Sandy called the governor and stated that it looked like a "pile of cat shit!"
The next day it was a different color.

Which reminds me of Stanfield's favorite story. Half of it is true, I made up the other half. I'll leave it to you to decide which is which.

People would always ask us if Sandy had any political clout. Stanfield would laugh and say, "Ask Mike."

So, they would ask me, and I'd tell them the story of Sandy getting out of a boat one day when she slipped on the gunnel and fell on the deck. "SHIT!" she screamed.

Then I just smile and finish the story, "I looked around and three people had their drawers dropped and two of them were state employees."

Agnes and Liz nekkid in the kiddie pool

Ahh man, Noel and I were going out in the jeep to shoot hogs on the beach one night. Hogs are detrimental to loggerhead sea turtle nests. A raccoon will sniff out a nest and eat some of the eggs. Hogs will sniff out a nest and eat every egg! And go sniffing for more! For some reason, we drove by Liz and Eugene's house. It was almost dark, but not dark enough! We heard someone yell and stopped to see what they wanted. Liz and Agnes were "nekkid" in Liz's daughter's kiddie pool! D-r-u-n-k! Agnes and Liz worked for Mrs. West, the former owner of Ossabaw. They weren't spring chickens, and neither were what the drunkest male would consider attractive. I still have that horrible image imprinted on my brain.

USAF

This is a really, funny story.

Goin' Dialin'

Lisa, Ike and I were snoozing away one night at our house on Ossabaw. We were awakened around two in the morning by someone pounding on the back door.
"United States Air Force!" was what I heard someone yelling, loudly.

We were not accustomed to having visitors on the island, much less at two in the morning. I popped out of bed and checked the back door, sure enough, someone was yelling," United States Air Force!" at our back door, I thought I had dreamed that.

I opened the door; there were five guys in wetsuits standing on our back porch.
"May I help you?" I asked.

"We are looking for the Canoochee River."

"It ain't around here," was my sleepy reply, the cobwebs of sleep were slowly clearing. "Are you sure it's not the Ogeechee River you're looking for?"

"That's it!"

After talking to these guys, who were on a training mission and were dumped fifty miles offshore, with a chart, a flashlight and a compass and were expected to navigate the maize of creeks in Georgia, and find the Ogeechee River, in the dark. I felt sorry for them. We loaded up in my truck and went to find their boat. From the description they gave me, they had found Bradley Creek and ran until it narrowed and ended at a causeway and culvert on Willows Road. We found their boat, loaded it in the truck and delivered it and the crew to Torrey Landing.

"There is the Ogeechee River," I explained to them. They dumped the inflatable boat in the river and four of them dove overboard to hold the inflatable for the "officer" to board. I was impressed! I was impressed that they found Ossabaw Sound from fifty miles offshore with a compass, a flashlight and a chart after being dropped into the ocean in the dark. If they hadn't taken a left into Bradley Creek, they would have made it!

More Ossabaw Stories

Cougar on Ossabaw?

One of the artists visiting the island informed our biologist that he had seen a cougar in the marsh. "And are you positive it was a cougar?" Was Big Mac's first question.

"Yes! I've traveled all through the west and I know a cougar when I see one. I got several photographs," he replied.

Anyway, we laughed after he left and waited for the cougar photos for about six months. Finally, they came in the mail.

Goin' Dialin'

Big Mac opened the envelope and said," Yep, there it is, a coongar!" The "photo evidence" of the cougar was one of the fuzziest pictures I've ever seen, of a raccoon.

Biggest water moccasin you ever seen. (theen)

"Get your gun Pa!" Ricky shouted.
Roger said," What's the matter Ricky?"
"Just get your gun Pa, just get your gun! It's the biggest dang water moccasin I've ever theen in my life!"
It was a garter snake. Ricky panicked when he and Roger turned the aluminum boat over, and a snake slithered out of it.

I nearly died laughing.

Ricky was Roger's non-son. Roger complained that he had all these people calling him "Pa", when he had no children of his own. Ricky was some sixteen-year-old urchin that Roger had rescued, Roger was good about that. Ricky had a speech impediment that I really should not have made fun of, but, hey, I'm human.

Ricky was helping Roger and Stanfield do some electrical wiring one day. Ricky made the connections before Roger got there.

"Ricky, I don't think you connected that right."
"Well, it's been a long time since I done any electrical work Pa."

We rolled laughing! Ricky was maybe 15 or 16 years old. Which reminds me of the bumper sticker, "Hire a teenager while they still know everything!"

Barges, scows and other non-descript craft

Barges, scows and other non-descript craft is how the Coast Guard defines a lot of vessels in the USCG rules. Boy did we have one; we got the Sapelo Scout, about a sixty-foot steel hull barge with a propulsion unit attached. Gene L. delivered it and warned Stanfield and me that the steering was backwards.

"Say whut?" We asked.

"The steering is backwards. If you want to turn to the right, you have to turn the steering wheel left."

We were speechless. We just could not fathom how this "non-descript craft" had operated for so many years with such a basic defect!

Well, we ran it a couple of times to Vernon View, towed it with the Queenie Mae Williams and ran both wide open so that we could make more speed. After a few barge trips, we started planning modifications to the steering to make the da'gone thing steer in the correct direction. It didn't take long, you get two good ol' boys together on a project, and good things happen!

We came up with added chain to the steering and an idler sprocket to reverse the direction of the helm steering. We had it! This contraption handled like a dream when Stanfield and I got through with it!

Of course, after we made the modifications, they gave it to the Department of Transportation.
Bummer.

Sapelo Stories

Lisa, Ike and I moved to Sapelo Island in 1985, it was like moving to town after Ossabaw. When we left Ossabaw, the three of us took 33 percent of the population with us. Sapelo had a store, two churches and a population of around 100 at the time.

We moved into the Marsh Landing house, which is the first house you see after leaving the ferry dock, Marsh Landing. This is a cool old house, built around 1869 by Bourke Spaulding.

First night with Gene and Anthony "showing me around"1985.

My first night on Sapelo after taking the Vessel Captain 1 position, Gene (the island manager, who recruited me and hired me) and Anthony (the DNR mechanic) came and took me for a tour. It was dark, I'm not sure if it was deliberate or not but they took me on all the back roads. I was lost shortly after we left Marsh Landing House. I remember we came through a lot of bushes hitting the side of the truck and one of them declared that we were now in Hog Hammock.

I have lived on Sapelo now for thirty-three years and I still cannot exactly, with confidence, tell you how these guys got me there that night, unless it was over a now washed out causeway. This I suppose was my initiation to the island.

Sapelo Queen

Oh, I loved that boat, the Sapelo Queen. The "Queen", was a sixty-five-foot fiberglass hull boat, built in 1978. She was the first ferry that the state of Georgia had built for Sapelo Island. We had the Janet, a steel hull fifty something foot crew boat that was certified for fifty passengers, built in 1961 for R.J. Reynolds, Jr. The Queen was three decks, certified for one hundred forty-nine passengers. Powered by twin 12V71 Detroit Diesels, eight hundred fifty total horsepower. The Queen was a great boat; still running at Dafuskie Island South Carolina I'm told.

Detroit Diesels had that great sound when you cranked them in the morning, beellallum, beellalum, bellaluum,

bellaluum, bella...lum, lum, lum, lum, do I have that sound right Detroit guys? (Maybe not quite enough bellaluums)

The Queen was the only ferry boat that we had for many years. When I started running her, in 1984, oh man, Freddie T. and Tracy W. sure helped me get used to a twin-screw boat. There is much difference in running a single screw boat and a twin screw. Single screw boats don't handle nearly as well a twin screw. The problem is getting all that information into your brain, making the changes to get the boat to do what you want it to do. This may be corny, but I've described it as," Making the boat an extension of yourself." You want to pivot; you react to get the boat to do what you want it to do. In the beginning, you have to think about what you need to do to the controls, when you develop the skills that I am talking about, you don't have to think, it just comes naturally. The Queen was a great handling boat. I ran her more that fourteen thousand trips to Sapelo in my time. Miss her!

Well You Know Things Happen

My bad, things happen. Love grows cold. I can make a lot of excuses that we got married too young, etc.
Lisa and I divorced in 1991.

Goin' Dialin'

But sometime in that same year, I was working with Captain Jim Whitted on the Sea Dawg. Jim and I were making the ferry runs to Sapelo during the spring break when we always took the Sapelo Queen to dry dock. I was there as a deckhand to make sure the DNR guidelines for priority passengers was followed.

I stopped this lady, quite nice-looking lady I might add, and told her that she could not come aboard with the open beer. I told her to dump it overboard and toss the can in the trash. I noticed the camera that she had and asked if she was "into photography". She said she was, I told her that I was doing a slideshow at the Marine Institute the next night and that she was invited. I advised the attractive lady that it was not advisable to wear socks at the slideshow since they would be "knocked off". Was I cocky or what?

Well, actually, I did knock her socks off, can't say I didn't warn her. Lucy and I became an item soon after that.

Dogs I Have Known

I stole that title from the late, great, Jerry Clower. Jerry was a great comedian and a great American.

"You ain't never been loved, 'til you have been loved by a dog."
Jerry Clower

Goin' Dialin'

The first dog I ever loved actually belonged to my older brother Johnny. He was an English setter that Johnny named "Bullet."

I've often said, of my childhood, that I remember getting Bullet, but I don't really remember anything before that particular event. I remember the first tooth that I lost, Bullet knocked loose with his paws jumping up on me.

Until I was seventeen years old, I always had Bullet. Just think about that, a child of four or five growing up with this dog around, he was always there, always extremely glad to see me. When I would get home from school, Bullet would run around and around the house barking, just so happy to see me. Unconditional love.

As I became a young man, Bullet became an old man.....Bullet died when I was seventeen. I remember the day well. It was a Saturday, I was building him a new doghouse. I kept looking over to where he was lying, I noticed that he wasn't flicking the annoying flies away with his tail or snapping at them with his mouth. I did not want to face the inevitable, I knew something was wrong. What I feared was that this friend that I'd had all my life was gone. He was.

Mama gave me a blanket to wrap him in. Daddy asked if I needed help. I declined the help and buried my childhood friend all by myself. I lined his grave with bricks that we had, but I wished for a permanent marker for my buddy, I never got that, meant to, it just didn't happen. Maybe it will someday.

Later in life, this love of this dog and the love from the dog somehow influenced me. Folks said that I needed a dog. "No, I don't need a dog!"

Cricket

When my son, Ike, was coming up, my then wife, Lisa, said that he needed a dog. I was reluctant, I had experienced the pain of losing a dog. I gave in and got a mixed breed, half golden retriever and half pit-bull, we named her Cricket.

Cricket was an amazing dog! She had instincts from both breeds that made her special. She could sniff out a raccoon, then she would chase and catch it! She had this amazing balance, she would ride in the back of my truck, climb up on the tool box for a better view and never, ever fell off. Corners, no problem. Sudden stops, no problem. Acceleration, no problem.

People would comment on her uncanny abilities to ride on my toolbox. "Does she ever slide off?"
"No."

She did have the raccoon addiction though. She would bail off the toolbox if she saw or smelled a raccoon, and

Goin' Dialin'

she would bring the raccoon to me whether I wanted it or not. Most of the time not.

I took her with me one day while I was going out to do some photography on the north end of Sapelo. By the time we got well up on the north end, I had totally forgotten she was back there on the toolbox. I saw a hawk fly across the road and light in a pine tree somewhere around Moses Hammock. I stopped, a ruckus ensued. Cricket either saw or smelled a raccoon and bailed off the toolbox. The hawk that I was going to photograph, casually flew away. There was all sorts of noise off in the bushes and Cricket came back to the truck with this really large raccoon "attached" to her face. I rolled up the window and locked the truck door!

She must have paid attention to Ike and me listening to Jerry Clower stories. Remember the "Knock him out John" story, where John Eubanks and the lynx were fighting in the top of the tree and John kept screaming, "Shoot this thang, have mercy, this thangs killin' me. Just shoot up here among us, one of us got to have some relief!"

But Cricket didn't realize that I had brought camera equipment, no gun. I yelled from the truck, "You got yourself into this, now get yourself out!"

Somehow, she got that big raccoon off her face and got back into the truck, I drove down the road for about a quarter mile and stopped and checked on her. She was fine, actually, quite happy!

Another near miss for Cricket was on Horse Pasture Road. I used to have a ten-speed bicycle on Sapelo and I biked to Nanny Goat Beach and back home most every evening, before I got too old and broken up that is. We met up with Owen and Jackie, they had stopped to watch a really big alligator crawl across the road. Well Cricket had to explore, she ran ahead of me despite all of my screaming, "NO,NO,NO!!" I just knew she was a goner. Owen saw the whole thing, he said she jumped on the alligator's back. Then she "levitated" about three feet in the air, turned and left.

Well, I was relieved and surprised that I still had a dog to finish my ride.

Cricket later died of natural causes. It was a sad day, she died on the fourth of July. Ike really missed that dog and I did too. Ike was five years old or so when we got Cricket, so I guess Cricket was Ike's "Bullet". He has always looked for a dog like Cricket, and there was never a replacement.

Logan

My wife's oldest son was moving to an apartment in Atlanta, to continue his education and he had a job. That's the kind of son to have right there, I don't care who you are.

Goin' Dialin'

His dilemma was that this apartment complex did not allow dogs. He had this BIG golden retriever name Logan. Logan was a great dog! Big golden with that large square head, a great friend to have. Logan never met a stranger, shared his big ol' love with anyone he met.

Well, Nat asked his mom to take Logan to Sapelo, she was not happy about that. Lucy would complain about buying dogfood, vet bills, etc. She said she was going to send these bills to Nat, I don't think that ever happened. I laugh about that today, I laughed about it about three months after Nat left Logan with us. We loved that dog! If Nat had asked her to return Logan, there would have been a fight.

Years went by, tennis balls were thrown and worn completely out. Lucy called me one day and said the vet told her that Logan had cancer. The poor old fella, we had to help him into the back of the truck, where he used to jump in, no problem. When she gave me that news, I went to the grocery store and bought the largest T-bone steak they had. Logan scarfed that down so fast, well he's a golden, they are gluttons! I said, "Dang buddy, did you even taste that?"

Logan died while Lucy was driving back from Florida, she called me in tears, of course, then I was in tears. We buried him under the live oak tree in our yard.

Goin' Dialin'

Levi

Levi was mine and Lucy's second golden retriever. He was a rescue dog. Lucy, who is a writer, wrote many articles for the Darien News, had to write an essay on why she wanted this dog. I was off tug boating at the time and Lucy needed company. She got the dog, surprise, surprise, she's a writer, she can write an essay for crying out loud. She went by my mom's house and said she needed a name for this new dog. My mom, in one of her last lucid moments, said, "Levi."

Levi was a great dog. Needless to say for golden retrievers, they are fantastic dogs.

There is one thing you cannot do with a golden, and that is take him fishing. If you are fishing from the bank or dock, he will jump in and try to bring your cork back to you. I took Levi with me in the boat once, never again! I had to drag his big muddy self-back into the boat. Me, dog and boat were a mess!

Levi loved people, like Logan, he never met a stranger. We would take him on the ferry, he would have to meet all the people on the ferry. He would have to get petted by all the passengers, everybody loved him.

Over the years, tennis balls were thrown, tennis balls were worn out.

Levi had that "Golden Retriever Problem"

He was a glutton, like all goldens. We had put a plastic bag full of chicken parts in the trash and he got into it while we were gone. He ate it bag and all, it killed him.

NOTHING LIKE STEPPING ON A SNAKE IN THE MIDDLE OF THE NIGHT

Do you want to wake up fast?
Just step on a snake in the bathroom. Whew! That'll wake you up. When Ike and I were living at Marsh Landing, I woke up and headed to the bathroom one night, barefoot. I didn't turn any light on because I knew the way and didn't want to completely wake up.

Well, I felt that cold squishy feeling under my right foot, which caused me to wake up completely! It was that "You have stepped on a reptile!" feeling. I went to squalling, flipped on the light and yep, a snake!

Ike was up in no time and we chased that stupid snake around the house until he left. We discovered that he had fallen into the house through the chimney, a perfect imprint of the snake was in the ashes.

What kind of snake was it you may ask. Probably a harmless garter snake or red rat snake, it could have been a cotton mouth timber rattler for all I know. When you step on it at one AM it just doesn't matter. You just want it GONE!

Goin' Dialin'

Tug boating

I was sitting in Dr. B's waiting room one morning in 2003. I picked up the Savannah Morning News and was just looking through it. A classified ad caught my eye, Tug Boat Captain Wanted, apply at Savannah Marine Services. There was also another sentence in there that said, "If you have never operated a tug boat, do not apply." Interesting, kind of made me wonder if people applied that had no experience.

I kissed Lucy goodbye, and said," Wow, I'm nervous." She wanted to know why, and I told her that I am used to being the guy with the answers, now I'm the guy with the questions.

It was early February 2004, I retired from the State of Confusion, I mean State of Georgia, and started my new job with Savannah Marine Services (SMS) as a tug boat captain. I was familiar with Savannah Marine's repair department since they had been doing our barge maintenance for us for many years. I was kinda new at this real tug boat business, but I wanted to go places and see things I hadn't seen. With DNR, we always had relatively short runs with the barges. Our "tug boats" were always converted boats such as the Zapala which was originally a trawler yacht.

Goin' Dialin'

The owner's son, William, oversaw the tugboat side of the business and he is one hard working sonafagun. William has an engineering degree and it showed. When we would do multiple barge tows he would give exacting instructions on which barge to place where and which one to ballast for the center of gravity to be in the perfect location for optimum handling.

My first gig with SMS, I was instructed to meet Captain Kirk on the tug Josiah Steven. I chuckled when William told me that on the phone, "You mean, Captain Kirk? Like the Starship Enterprise?"

Our tug crews consisted of four guys. Two licensed captains, one is the captain who works the six to twelve shifts, one is the mate and works the twelve to six shift AM and PM. The other two are deckhands, one is cook, the other is the engineer and in charge of the engine room. Being the new guy, I was the mate on this trip. William had told me that we were going to Green Cove Springs, Florida.

I got out my trusty charts and studied up on the route between Savannah and Green Cove Springs. My confidence level rose, yeah, I had traveled about half of that route. From Savannah to the Altamaha River. Most of my tug boating with DNR was on unmarked rivers, traveling on the Intracoastal Waterway was going to be a walk in the park, or so I thought.

I had the great honor of meeting Captain Kirk that night, not to be confused with Crazy Kirk of later stories.

Goin' Dialin'

Luckily, I brought a flashlight with me and when I got to the boat yard, I searched among the tugs until I found the Josiah Steven, hum.... Not as big as I thought. The Josiah was a fifty-five-foot, model bow tug. For you landlubbers, there are two types of tugs in the SMS fleet, model bows and push boats. A model bow tug has a bow like a typical boat except for a push knee that runs vertically from the water line up to the bow. A push boat has a squarer looking bow and usually has two push knees to "face up to" the barge. A push knee is a big chunk of steel covered in a rubber material.

Oh man, I was in boat heaven, steel boats, steel barges, steel touching steel touching water, Archimedes would be proud!

I was just hanging around waiting for something to happen. A little after midnight a pickup truck enters the boat yard, it got my attention because it was loaded with groceries. The kind of truck I like! A young fellow exited the driver's seat, "You must be Mike, the new mate."

Mate, whut? I've been Captain Mike for twenty years, was I downgraded? "Uh, yeah, I'm a captain, but I guess I am the new mate."

"Hey, glad to meet you." Shaking my hand, "I'm Jason, deckhand and chief cook."

"Very glad to meet you, Jason." That mate thing was still bothering me. Jason and Lee were the deckhands on

Goin' Dialin'

this trip, looking back, it never got better. Two seasoned, really good deckhands, on my maiden voyage with SMS. I worked with Lee on several trips, he was an excellent engineer, deckhand and friend. He had a massive heart attack and died two years later on a tug boat in the Gulf of Mexico, the crew did CPR, which we are all required to train for, but he didn't make it. They were working the Hurricane Katrina repairs, I remember that I was southbound around Dafuskee Island when William called me and told me of Lee's death, I couldn't believe it.

Anyway, back to that first night. Captain Kirk came out of his cabin, in his underwear, tighty whities, sans shirt. Kirk was seventy-three years old at that time. He seriously looked like the guy they copied to make Popeye the Sailor man. Huge forearms, sadly gravity was taking control of a lot of skin, but in remarkable shape for his age. He opens the corner of his mouth and in a raspy voice says," You must be Mike, but William said you were retarred, and you look too young to be retarred."

I answered in the affirmative and explained to Kirk that I had a good deal with the State of Georgia and was able to retire at the age of 45. Kirk gave me the rundown on the electronics, steering system etc. He had cussing down to a fine art. After going over the radar, depth finder and such he said," And there's that bleep, bleep, bleep computer, ya can use it if you want to but I'd like to throw the whole bleep, bleep, bleep......bleep thang overboard! Bleeping thang ain't got no bleeping bidness on a bleeping tug boat."

We got underway, "Security Call, tug Josiah Steven departing Savannah Marine, light boat, outbound Savannah River to Field's Cut." Huh? Captain Kirk's security call on channel 13 got my attention. (Security calls are always given to alert other vessels of our presence on the waterway and our intent. In ports like New York, you have traffic control which does this for you.)

"Uh, Cap, I was told we were going to Green Cove." That would be south. Field's Cut is north.

"Naw, we're going to bleeping Charleston, pick up some bleeping dredge pipe, money bleeping talks ya know."

"Oh." Oh no, I've never been north of the Savannah River and its dark!

Well, at least we were light boat, which means it was only the tug, no barge. Lee and I messed with the computer program most of the night, until I got the hang of finding the Intracoastal Waterway charts. Right click, who would have thunk it? The ICW charts have the magic "magenta line" marking the waterway from Miami to Maine. Lee made lots of coffee for me that night. By zero six hundred, when Captain Kirk came to relieve me, we were in Beaufort, South Carolina. It was not only dark it had gotten foggy as well. I was used to such, as we ran in all conditions on the Sapelo Ferry. Well, Kirk immediately "pushed up to the bank."

Pushed up, is a tug boat term for, "whimped out." You push the boat or barge bow into the bank and add enough power to keep it there. I became very familiar with the term in the two years that followed. Really bad weather, bad currents, or if you are ahead of schedule, you "push up" and wait. I would learn to "push up" very soon. But Captain Kirk was old school; he just didn't trust all these newfangled things such as radar and GPS. The old guy taught me a lot, I can't knock him, he knew the ICW from Jacksonville to Norfolk, and never needed that "bleep bleep" computer that I relied on!

Wappoo Creek Bridge, a Hazard to Navigation

My first encounter with Wappoo Creek Bridge was on my first trip to Charleston with Captain Kirk. As described above, we were light boat; something that I learned early is that if you are "light boat" and had no barge, you cannot pass through some bridges that are on curfew. During rush hour, bridges will not open to you unless you have a tow, which is considered "restricted in your ability to maneuver." Bridges will then open for you at your request unless they have an EMS or other emergency pending. We were stuck waiting for the curfew to pass when Captain Reed called us.

Goin' Dialin'

Captain Reed was bringing the Sarah Kaitlin, our push boat, south bound with a three-hundred-foot barge and asked Kirk to wait and help him through Wappoo Creek Bridge because the Sarah Kaitlin had lost one rudder on this trip. Captain Kirk knew exactly what to do and I was very grateful he was there. When the Sarah Kaitlin came through the bridge, Captain Kirk made contact with the port side of the barge and pushed it perfectly to line up, this was all done in the dark. I was impressed. But recall, this was my first trip north of the Savannah River. When we finally went through the bridge, I realized how difficult that maneuver was. I had not seen the northern side of the bridge. I was soon introduced to how difficult that bridge is to navigate even with both rudders intact.

Something about engineers, roads and bridges, why do they always put bridges on the curves of rivers? Very few are located on straight parts of creeks or rivers, and if they are on a straight part, the fender system of the bridge is set at an angle? Are they trying to make this hard for us, or are they just sadistic, sick little rascals?

Wappoo Creek Bridge is on a curve in the creek; Elliot's cut is a canal that they cut from Wappoo Creek to the Stono River on the south end. Charleston Harbor, the Ashley River is on the north end. The current really races through there. When we would leave Savannah, we would draw a route to Wappoo on the computer program, and time the arrival for the least amount of current. We would time Wappoo Bridge and Elliot's Cut to be reached on a "head tide," meaning the tide was

Goin' Dialin'

coming toward us, you have more control of the tow when the tide is coming toward you, versus a "fair tide," when the tide is on your stern pushing you. It makes a ton of difference in the handling of the tow.

On my first trip northbound with a barge, Bobby Moore was the captain and I was the mate, Bobby was retired from the US Coast Guard. He was the guy that installed and repaired the markers on the ICW; he knew what he was doing. He showed me that you had to hug the port side of the bridge fender system, and then give all the rudder you have to port, and just clear the starboard fender with the stern of the boat. Worked like a charm, I had northbound down!

Southbound was more difficult. Especially with an empty barge, which will slide. Loaded barges have more maneuverability; they sit lower in the water and have more grab. Empty barges sit high in the water and have less grab. Empty barges, those that are two hundred to three-hundred-foot-long, are difficult to get though Wappoo Bridge southbound.

After sliding into the fender system of the bridge twice, and each time, if you even touch a piling with the tug or barge, they call out the marine surveyors, divers, etc. They call you on the radio, get your name, company name and all of that and send the company a bill for the survey, and any damage that they claim was done. All this is done on the VHF radio and humiliating because all boaters in the area hear this. It's not a private conversation by any means.

Goin' Dialin'

Well after about a year of dreading Wappoo Bridge, I had the opportunity of going southbound with Captain Kirk. We were at our shift change, I asked Kirk to give me some pointers on Wappoo Bridge.

"Well," he said, out of the corner of his mouth in his raspy voice," Let me just show you how I do it." And he did, it was a work of art! "You want to get way over to port." He ran slap over a "no wake" buoy and spit pieces of it out of the stern of the boat. "That bleeping thing is in the way, don't pay no attention to the bleeping no wake buoy, that ain't even legal. Don't know why they let 'em put crap like that in our way," He turned the empty three-hundred-foot barge toward the bridge and it lined up perfectly, didn't even slow down, it was just perfect! I was impressed, and I learned a lot, from the master!

Deckhands

I retired from the state of Georgia in 2004 and started running tugboats until 2006. I told my wife, Lucy, that I wanted to tugboat for two years to pay off Ike's college debts and to see the USA.

I met several of my goals, went to Maine, went to New Orleans and ran on the Mississippi River. Went through New York several times, up the East River to Long Island Sound, passed under the Brooklyn Bridge and by the Statue of Liberty. Went to New Jersey, New Hampshire, Rhode Island, Connecticut, Massachusetts, went through the Cape Cod Canal a couple of times. Delivered dredging supplies to Nassau Bahamas, traveled across Florida via the Okeechobee waterway, a beautiful trip.

Several of those trips were with very good deckhands, most were not.

Smoked Bacon

We were making a trip to Norfolk VA with a load of concrete bridge beams on the Sarah Kaitlin, a push boat. I came down from the wheelhouse; you had to exit the wheelhouse outside and walk down three flights of stairs to get to the galley.
When I opened the galley door, smoke was boiling out. I asked the deckhand what he was burning, he said, and I kid you not, "this is smoked bacon, it's supposed to smoke like that."

Hot Dogs

One thing tug boats are famous for is the food, we did eat well. If you had a deckhand who could cook, you kept that information to yourself. Other captains in the company would steal a good cook faster than a cop can eat a donut. I learned that the hard way.

Goin' Dialin'

Before a long trip we would fill up grocery carts full of food, I once spent 5 hours at Wal-Mart in Savannah, 9:00 pm until 2:00 am, had six carts of groceries, the bill was a little under two grand.

Well, we had all this good, fresh food and what does the deckhand do? Heats frozen pizza for dinner. I brushed that off because the deckhands had worked hard that day making up a difficult tow. The next evening, I asked the deckhand what was for dinner, he said," hotdogs." I laughed; I seriously thought he was kidding. It reminded me that the Braves were playing (you know, baseball, hotdogs, they go together) started tuning the radio and forgot all about hotdogs.

On our tugs we always had four guys, the captain the mate and two deckhands. Sometimes I was the captain, sometimes the mate; it depended on the seniority of the crew. This time I was the mate.

Well, Captain Stanley came up to the wheelhouse to check on where we were, what's coming up and such. Stanley asked me, "What's for dinner?"

I said," Hotdogs."

Stanley said, well I won't repeat what Stanley said. It was not at all nice.

When I got off from my watch, I went to the galley and the deckhand was cooking steaks. When he got through, we were going through Thunderbolt, GA; the deckhand

Goin' Dialin'

flagged down a small boat, threw his duffel on and left. We had to pick up another deckhand at Skidaway Bridge.

One thing about deckhands, I never was rude to the deckhand that was cooking my food, Stanley was, no telling what Stanley got in his meals. Something to think about.

Tighty Whities

My boss with Savanna Marine was named William; he was the company owner's son. He was one hard working son of a gun. His dad, Joe had instilled hard work into him as a youngster, and William absolutely loved tug boating.
I was running the Josiah Steven, (all the boats were named after Joe's grandchildren) south from Savannah and got to Skidaway River when I stopped. There was a sailboat race going on right slap dab across the Intra Coastal Waterway! Blow boats everywhere. Well, William was awakened because I stopped. He came up to the wheelhouse in his underwear, tighty whities, and I must admit they were better than the turquoise bikini underwear that the 73-year-old Captain Kirk wore, but that's another story.

"What's going on?" he asked.

"A da'gone regatta!" was my reply.

Goin' Dialin'

"They can't do that! They can't block the ICW!" He proceeded to take the helm and just sort of charge his way through the sailboats.

I covered my face, just knew that WTOC was filming this! Idiot in tug boat breaks up regatta, film at 11!

Several of the sail boaters raised a middle finger for some reason.

Crazy Kirk, Ivan and Glenn

Oh man, this is a story with Chapters!

We had this one couple, man and wife, Ed and Edie who were both tugboat captains and worked together. I never got to know them very well because they always worked together, captain and mate. We were prepping the tugs, everybody getting water, oil, fuel, groceries, etc. I had a few minutes and went over to Ed and Edie's boat. They'd heard that I was taking Crazy Kirk as my mate on this run. I asked," Why do they call him Crazy Kirk?"

Because he's crazy, was their reply. And so, I asked if they meant like quirky, like most tug boat captains. They said no, he's certified, has papers to prove he's crazy! Oh Boy, a trip to Philadelphia with a nut case. Just exactly how I wanted this trip to start. Add in Ivan,

Goin' Dialin'

poor Ivan was not the sharpest knife in the drawer, my new deckhand.

I, unfortunately, was the captain on this trip, Crazy Kirk was my mate. I took Ivan on my watch, because I felt sorry for him and knew Kirk wouldn't have the patience that I have. Glenn was a seasoned deckhand and I figured he and Kirk would get along fine.

It all went ok, from Savannah to Norfolk, no problems, I was feeling good. We delivered the barge to Norfolk, picked up another and headed up the Chesapeake Bay to Philly. That's when it all went terribly wrong.

Kirk came up to the wheelhouse, just irate! Ivan had not replaced the toilet paper roll in the head. You need to fire him! OK, just let me pull over and drop him off somewhere.

Ivan came up to the wheelhouse contemplating suicide. I managed to talk him out of that. Apparently, he and Kirk had other altercations sometime during the day because Ivan came up to the wheelhouse and announced that he quit. He took his suitcase out on the barge and kicked back in a dredge pipe.

I called Glenn and got him to take a sandwich out to Ivan and lure him back on the tug.

Ivan informed me that he had lost his wallet on the barge somewhere, so he didn't have ID on him.

Goin' Dialin'

Another day went by, quietly, I'm enjoying heading north in the Chesapeake, just doesn't get any better than this….. Kirk comes to the wheelhouse and informs me that Ivan didn't wash the dishes in the time frame that Kirk allowed. "You need to FIRE HIM! Yadda, Yadda, Yadda." I informed Kirk that we had this barge in front of us. It's kind of hard to pull over at the next marina and discharge a deckhand. Besides, he doesn't even have ID; you can't even get on a bus without ID! And he's not very smart. I refused to fire him. Kirk mumbled and headed downstairs.

I walked down to the galley after my watch, looked at Glenn and asked if he knew that he and I were the sane ones on this trip. He replied yes, he knew, I asked if he knew how scary that was, and he replied, "OH yeah."

Believe it or not, we made it to Philly, dropped off that barge and headed back to Norfolk, without incident I'd like to add.

We spent the night tied up at the dredge company in Norfolk. The next morning, we got underway; Ivan called me on the intercom and informed me that he had been bitten by a brown recluse spider.

I asked him how he was so sure, he said that a friend of his was bitten and this looked the same. After talking to my boss, William, on the bag phone, which is what we had in 2005, William wanted me to look at the actual rash…..I told him I'd rather not.

Goin' Dialin'

Anyway, Ivan recovered from the rash, which wasn't a brown recluse bite. The next night Ivan called me on the intercom... "I'm having chest pains and having trouble breathing!" I told him to take two aspirin and call me in the morning.

About two weeks later, we were getting tug boats ready to go out, Ivan was on another boat, he came over and asked me if he "bothered me on that trip to Philly"

I looked at poor Ivan and said, "Bothered me, you threatened suicide, quit, got bitten by a brown recluse, and had a heart attack. Why on earth would you think that bothered me?"

Morehead City Bridges

There's a double bridge in Morehead City North Carolina, a highway bridge and a railroad bridge. I was running through there one night in very rough weather, my boss, William was on this trip. This was my test and William wanted to see if he could sleep at night while myself and others did similar trips. The tow was a 300-foot barge loaded with 6 million pounds of pre-stressed concrete bridge girders. We had six trips to do so William wanted to find out if I was capable of doing it. Savannah Georgia to Norfolk Virginia.

I was crabbing, the only way I know to describe it, up to the bridge's fender system. William came up to the wheelhouse, and said that he thought that I'd be at this bridge soon. I said, "Yeah, we're in it." He asked if I had my deckhand on the barge with a radio, I told him no, I wasn't going to put a green deckhand on the barge to panic when he saw the approach I was making, it was like a 45 degree angle to the fender system.

He said," Good decision." My deckhand had been working at Wal-Mart only three days before.

My Eureka Moment

I was talking to a deckhand, don't remember his name, it gets that way. You go through so many that they start blending together. This was actually a good deckhand, and we did have those, the bad ones with issues and funny stories are the ones that are remembered. I do remember that we had many good conversations during our watch.

We were going north on one of the six trips from Savannah to Norfolk, with the 300-foot barge loaded with six million pounds of pre-stressed concrete bridge girders. (We were contracted to do six trips, I think I was the only one who did them all.)

We averaged three miles per hour. If you decided to stop, it took over 30 seconds to bring that tow to a stop, not something that you want to get complacent about. I was working the Mate's watch, 12:00 to 6:00, am and pm. Our captain was Captain Kirk, (not Crazy Kirk, different captain) yeah, like the starship Enterprise. Kirk was seventy-three years young at the time, had arms like Popeye the Sailorman. Kirk had been running tugs since way before I was born, he taught me a lot and it was always a pleasure to work with him.

We had gotten past my favorite river on the Intra Coastal Waterway, the Wacamaw River in South Carolina, always the most beautiful part of the trip. We were making our way north through the "Rock Pile", which is the canal cut through rock inland of Myrtle Beach, South Carolina. The canal is narrow; there are always either rocks or docks on both sides.
My deckhand and I were conversing earlier in the day, about all the tugboat captains and their strange, quirky habits and ways.

Well, I was in the "Rock Pile" it was 4 am, dark, and it suddenly got foggy, seriously foggy! It all hit me at once, the "quirky" captains, and so much craziness. I hit my self-upside the head and shouted," You have to be crazy to do this!" It all made sense after that.

New Orleans and Cajuns

On another trip we stopped in New Orleans to get an engine fixed that was under warranty.

Goin' Dialin'

We went through Commercial Lock, I had to converse with the first Cajun that I'd ever encountered, he had that great accent, but I understood everything he said. We ran up the Mississippi River a little way and went up some canal. After tying up in the canal, the mechanic showed up. He checked the engine over said something and left. He came back the next day with a helper and they fixed the engine. Meanwhile my boss called from Savannah and asked me what the mechanic found wrong. I told him that I had no idea. He got a little peeved with me and wanted to know if I even talked to the mechanic. I told him yes, I even asked the guy what he found, but I could not understand a word he said!

Later, the mechanic gave me work order with everything written down. I called the boss and told him, they replaced the pistons and liners, funny the guy could write it down, but I could not understand what he said! Anyway, my boss was laughing about it by the time we were leaving. That guy was a Real Cajun!

Fishing can be Dangerous!

Fish hook in the head

My ex-wife and I went fishing at Gary Hole, on Sapelo one afternoon. We were fishing with bottom rigs and dead bait for redfish. Gary Hole is waaay out in the marsh, it's a trek and you must walk about a quarter of a mile through the marsh to get there. We got there and

Goin' Dialin'

started fishing, she reared back to cast and caught the hook in my scalp. Broke a thirty-pound test leader setting the hook in my head.

I had a hat on, the hook went through the hat and pinned it on my head! The shrimp was still on the hook, I managed to get the shrimp off. We both tried to get the hook out of my head but gave up. "We need to go to the emergency clinic." I said. Which I knew would be embarrassing because I had been there only two weeks before.

We bought a "Slip and Slide" for Ike a couple of weeks earlier, of course I did not read the directions. I did later and the very first item was to check the site and make sure that there are no sharp objects as they will cut through the plastic and the idiot sliding on it. Well, I managed to find a piece of glass with my knee and had to go to the emergency clinic and get it sewn up.

So, after a quarter mile marsh hike, drive home to get keys and driver's license, seven mile boat trip to the mainland and a thirty mile drive to Brunswick to Glynn Immediate Care, we arrived.

"Mr. Sellers!" I am now greeted by name by the receptionist. Great.

"Well, I usually take my hat off, but it is pinned to my head by a fishhook." I calmly replied.

Goin' Dialin'

The poor receptionist was trying to hide the laughter that was bubbling up inside of her. She looked as though she had a nervous tic she was trying hard to control. She took my information and asked me to wait over there.

My name was called, and I walked back to the examination room. A few minutes later, the doctor came in, stinking of gin and proceeded to lie on the table. Sorry that was from the Beatles "Rocky Raccoon."

No, the doctor came in looked at the hat and fishhook, and said," I've got to think about this for a few minutes."

Several minutes later he came back in the room with a pair of lineman's pliers, a pair of needle nose pliers and a LARGE syringe.

I said," Those don't look like surgical instruments Doc, did you have to go to your truck to get them?" He was amused.

He used the lineman's pliers to snip off the eye of the hook and removed my hat. He proceeded to take the large syringe and stick it in my scalp.

He left and after another several minutes, he returned, took the needle nose pliers, popped the hook through my scalp, cut off the barbed end of the hook and threaded it back through my scalp and declared," All Done!"

I am still cautious about fishing with other people.

Goin' Dialin'

Fishing alone can just as bad...

I went to Boll Weevil Plantation for a few days back in the early 1990's, to visit my good friend, Jim Evans. Jim and his family lived on Sapelo Island in the 1980's and we became very close friends.

Jim had an airplane when he lived on Sapelo that he totally rebuilt, a Piper Pacer, a rag wing tail dragger. We would fly around Sapelo and he flew us to Macon on one occasion. We were flying along, IFR, (I fly roads) and Jim would suddenly jerk forward and look down as if he were in a panic. I kept thinking that something was wrong. I would ask, and Jim would tell me that everything was fine. He jerked forward again, and I said," Jim, you do that crap one more time and I'm going to slap you silly!" He laughed and said that he didn't mean to scare me.

Well, Jim had work to do during the day as manager of Boll Weevil, a quail hunting plantation and suggested that I try to catch a bass at Long Pond. Folks that know me know that you don't have to twist my arm very hard to get me to go fishing. I had a great time at Long Pond. I caught several small bass and released them. I was using a bang-a-lure which has two sets of treble hooks.

I caught this small bass, probably one pound, when I lifted him into the boat to release him; he flipped and managed to get the other set of treble hooks into his tail. At this point, I had a live spring. He was bent as far as he could bend with one set of hooks in his mouth and the other in his tail. I worked and worked and finally got his tail freed, and then he did what fish do, flipped. This landed the free set of treble hooks into the second joint of my right-hand ring finger, past the barb of the hook.

OK, now I have this dilemma, I have a lure with two sets of hooks, I have a lively bass on one set of hooks and the other set is buried in my finger joint. This fish is going wacko, and the louder I scream the more wacko he goes. I don't think I even have to mention how painful this all is. I finally managed to get the fish off the hook and back into the pond, this was no small accomplishment! Then I was vacillating on whether to go to the hospital, emergency clinic, wherever, or try to get this hook out myself.

I removed the hook myself, all I could think of was the pain and how far from medical help I was, and the time involved in getting this da'gone thing out of my finger! I finally got it loose. Whew!

So, fishing can be dangerous, even when you are alone.

Mother Mother ocean

As Jimmy Buffet said:
Mother mother ocean

Goin' Dialin'

I've heard you call
Wanted to puke upon your waters
Since I was three feet tall

Or something like that.

This is really embarrassing for a boat captain to admit, but I get seasick! Ike and I went out one morning to K reef. We had his friend Rim with us, pronounced Reem. I used to say Rim, as in wheel rim. Ike kept correcting me on this and we decided to name her Lug Nut.

Anyway, Ike, Rim and I were out at K reef, catching black bass and I was busy vomiting over the side of the boat and fell overboard. Ain't hard to do folks. Ike looks over and says, "You better get your butt back in the boat, a barracuda would like that shinny watch you have on! Not to mention all the chum you've put in the water."

I drug myself back into the boat, and we decided to leave. Meanwhile, Lug Nut was looking good on the bow of the boat in her bikini.

Ike threw a lure out as we idled away, a fifty-pound cobia latched on to the lure and we drug him aboard. Ike was getting the lure out of his mouth when somehow, he flipped and caught the hook in Ike's finger joint. Dilemma, Ike kept asking me to get this dad gone thing out of his finger, I kept insisting we go to the emergency clinic. I finally held my breath and took needle nosed pliers and jerked it out of his finger joint. I swear it hurt worse than when I did it to myself at Long Pond. The things we do for our children.

Ike and I purchased that boat mostly with money he made working during summer vacation. He always wanted to get into offshore fishing. Me, I'm a creek and sound guy myself. I'm perfectly happy fishing inshore.

The first morning that we went fishing offshore was to Grey's Reef, twenty miles east of Doboy Sound. We rose early that morning, I grabbed a loaf of bread, a knife and jar of peanut butter in case we got hungry.

The first lesson I learned about offshore fishing in a twenty-foot boat; it is impossible to hold on to the railing with one hand and make a peanut butter sandwich with the other. It just can't be done.

UP BARN CREEK WITHOUT A PADDLE

My old boss, Big Mac called me and asked if I could help his friend who was starting hunting and fishing magazine get some saltwater, coastal articles in Georgia. This was one weekend when Murphy's Law took effect and everything that could go wrong, did.

I had told them about stalking tailing redfish in the marsh, and of course, casting for shrimp with a cast net. Two of my favorite activities on the coast, well before I

Goin' Dialin'

got too old and broken up. Redfish will get vertical in the marsh, to bottom feed on crabs and shrimp, when they do, their tail appears on the surface.

To be assured of catching redfish, you need fresh bait, mullet to be exact. These folks were arriving on the 3:30 ferry and I went to catch bait before they got there. I took off in my little fourteen-foot boat up Barn Creek to catch fresh mullet for the later afternoon high tide, when you find redfish in the marsh. I was zipping along when my hat blew off my head, I was feeling young and invincible, and cranked the tiller on the 15 HP motor all the way over to the left, to just kind of whip around in the narrow creek and do a 180, like I'd done many times before. Hey, it was a good hat, I wanted to keep it. Well, that turned out to be my first mistake of the day! The motor hit something under the water and jumped off the transom. I managed to hold on to the fuel line, as I watched the motor sink into the creek. I distinctly remember the smoke bubbles coming up out of the water as the motor died, and holding on to the only lifeline, the fuel line. I gently pulled on the fuel line, to try and lift the motor enough where I could grab hold of something more substantial. The fuel line slipped off! Bye, bye motor! I quickly paddled to the bank and stuck the paddle in the mud to mark where the motor was approximately located. I waded and waded through the creek until I finally stepped on the motor, dove down into the creek and retrieved it. I hung it back on the transom, loosely, and grabbed the paddle which had been previously driven in the mud to mark the location. I pried between the bow and the paddle to free the little boat from the bank, I broke the paddle.

OK, so now I'm up Barn Creek without a paddle. I tied the bowline to my belt and waded to Barn Creek dock, a trek, I tied a rope to the motor and dumped it back in the water, air is what causes corrosion problems later. By this time, it's nearly boat time and I had to go meet my guests at the dock or be late.

So, I appear, to my former boss and his friend, the publisher, at the dock, soaked, muddy, a mess! And with no fresh bait! I got them settled at my house and explained what happened, and that I have a motor to flush out and soak down with oil this evening instead of fishing. Well, they chipped in and helped get the motor cleaned up, but these were the days before electronic ignition and I could not get the motor running that night.

So, we fished the morning tide, with frozen mullet (not as good as fresh) didn't even see a redfish tailing, one of those nothing mornings! Then we hit the sound at low tide in my 18-foot boat, not my choice of boats for shrimp casting, caught a few shrimp and by then I think the whole bunch had totally lost confidence in my abilities.

Well, Sunday came, their day of departure. It was raining. I went on my first boat run to pick up my brother and his family. I went to tie my boat at Marsh Landing alongside the UGA's boat and slipped on the bow deck and fell overboard. The late Cracker Johnson was there on the dock and yelled at some UGA guys to, "Fish that white boy out of the river!" They did. So, I appear at my house, soaked, just as I met my guests. They were not impressed! So, goes the life of an islander.

My old crate

When I started running the Sapelo Queen back in 1984, (I actually started as a Vessel Captain I in 1985, but I had to run it some to upgrade my Coast Guard License in 1984) I couldn't see over the dash of the wheelhouse. The captains, Freddie Todd and Tracy Walker, were over 6 feet tall. I'm not going to share how tall (or short) I am but I'm not six foot! I found a Canada Dry crate, a wooden one, the old style which American Pickers would now like, and I would stand on it while I docked and undocked the Queen. I actually had input when we built the Annemarie and insisted that the dash be shorter than the Queen. I have many stories about my crate.

My best friend, Jerry, was apt to hide my crate from me. He, and the "girls" (Ginger G., Donna P. and Jane B.) thought that it was hilarious. I started locking the wheelhouse after the first time. Okay I forgot to lock it a few times; crate is nowhere to be found. I found it on top of the wheelhouse usually.

We had a new manager for the Senior Citizens Center on Sapelo named Adrienne, she started her job while Tracy was on duty (we worked seven days on and seven off), and she quietly wondered why Tracy had that crate in the way while he ran the boat. I came in for my shift and wondered why this gal was snickering....she said," Poor thing, I wondered why Tracy had that crate in the way! I see you need it to see over the dash!"

My best friend Jerry again. We went to Lake Lanier fishing for a week. Two of his brothers lived at Gainesville, Georgia and we went after crappie. My first day there his brother comes out with this gigantic, plastic Coke crate, so I could see over the side of the boat. Ha Ha! Very Funny! I paid them back by catching more crappie than they did (that's my story and I'm sticking to it!).

The Queen was sold to entities on Dafuskie Island a few years ago; I guess my old crate went with it.

Microwave and TV

Many years ago, Larry Johnson and I built an addition to the wheelhouse of the Sapelo Queen. The reason was to convert the vessel into a multiuse boat. We had three boats at that time, the Queen, the Annemarie and the Zapala. The Zapala was a confiscated yacht that we acquired from the UGA Marine Institute and it served as our tugboat.

Goin' Dialin'

The Queen was our backup ferry. Well, I had the great idea that we could use the Queen for towing and backup ferry and get rid of the Zapala. Boating folks know that boats are, "Holes in the water, in which you pour money." We could save lots of money by getting rid of one.

Bob M. was our regional supervisor at the time and he believed in Larry's and my abilities. We engaged a naval architect and satisfied the Coast Guard with drawings and other promises that we would have a new "stability test" after the modifications. I submitted the naval architects drawings and my drawings of the electrical system to the USCG and finally,,,and I mean Finally, things were approved. (This was like half the battle, getting funding and USCG approval, what a nightmare!)

Larry showed up to start the modifications with a level and a framing square. I asked him where are you going to use those? Larry was great; he laughed and said," I'm a carpenter!" I replied that level and square have no business on a boat! We eyeballed the curve of the existing wheelhouse lines, put some marks on the deck and got started. The higher ups in the DNR came by from time to time, it took us a few months to get this project done, and they were impressed! David W., our director, was impressed with the wiring; Todd H. was impressed with the fiberglass work. (I had to show him the infrared thermometer I used and the chart of how much hardener, according to temperature that you mixed with the resin.)

Goin' Dialin'

Larry and I did the whole thing, even the guys at the boatyard were impressed, said that it looked like the boat was made that way! Larry taught me several things, like building countertops with Formica, gluing them to plywood with contact cement. The only thing we really had problems with was the Lexan windows; we decided that if we were to undertake such a project again, we'd farm out the windows.

I told you that story to tell you this one.

Well, she was done. I told Bob that we needed a microwave and a TV to finish our accomplishment. I was later informed that we could not buy either as per state regulations.

Enter Chris. We needed a paint job on the Annemarie. I had a big chunk of money set aside for this project. I approached Chris who ran the boatyard, "We need a TV and a microwave out of this chunk of money." No problemo, here's $300.00, go get what you need. I was nervous, Chris, dang, don't hand over cash like that to me, I was looking around and feeling guilty! I went to Wal-Mart, bought a TV, microwave and added about twenty bucks and got a boom box to boot!

Bob asked me later, "How'd you get that microwave, TV and boom box?"
My answer," Do you really want to know?"

He said no, just wondered.

Goin' Dialin'

Tug Boating, the beginning.....

Not long after I had started running the Sapelo Ferry, Freddie T. asked me if I wanted to get some tug boat experience and go on the fuel barge runs to Ossabaw. I jumped at the opportunity. This started when C.V. was regional supervisor, in later years Bob M. was regional supervisor and he had to ask why Freddy took me and a UGA employee on these trips. I guess it smelled of a junket to him. Freddie responded that he was training me to take over when he retired. When Bob asked me, I explained that I keep the peace. Freddie and Stanfield P. would kill each other if I wasn't there to referee. They seriously would, Stanfield would accuse Freddie of not delivering the fuel they paid for, and Freddie would be adamant about the amount of fuel they delivered. Those two could argue till the cows come home.

On my very first trip, it was me, Freddie and Teddy B. An afternoon thunderstorm came up while we were underway, I innocently asked," What happens if lightning strikes this barge which has about six inches of gasoline in the bottom?"

"SHUT UP!!! SHUT UP!!! We don't discuss such as that!" They replied in stereo. So, I'm left thinking that maybe lightning would not be a good thing.

Goin' Dialin'

At that time, the Zapala belonged to the University of Georgia Marine Institute (UGAMI). In later years they transferred the tug and both barges to the DNR and we took over all the barging. I think that was around 1993. The fuel barge, properly called a "tank barge", was a single skin sixty-foot by twenty-foot barge which would carry about thirty thousand gallons of fuel. It had six compartments which we divided between diesel fuel and gasoline. The UGAMI would charter the boat and barge to us and provide an engineer to go with us. The Zapala was originally a trawler yacht, twin screw, fifty-five foot steel hull. For you gear heads, it was powered by two 471 Detroit Diesels and 2:1 Twin Disc Gears. Not a lot of power for a tug boat, but it was basically free. It was confiscated by Customs for having several tons of weed under the deck. They frown on that apparently. UGAMI acquired it in the eighties.

Now these were both my and Freddie's wilder days. I was the cook and would write up menus for the barge trips and buy groceries accordingly. We would usually have the top shelf of the fridge loaded with food; all the lower shelves were filled with beer, lots of beer. When we would tie up, the beer came out! I would painstakingly make these lists of food needed for the barge trips. Okay, breakfast, what do I want first thing in the morning, ... coffee, okay coffee on the list. Next, eggs, bacon, sugar for coffee, creamer, some people like creamer in their coffee. Toast, bread is a main ingredient! We will need that for sandwiches at lunch too. Add a couple of loaves of bread. Butter! Got to have that! I would sit and think of all the things that we

Goin' Dialin'

take for granted, we have those staples in the fridge kind of stuff that we would not have and not be able to obtain when out on the water for several days. This was a mental exercise I went through before every barge trip. Dinner, hum, fried pork chops, ok what do you need for fried pork chops? Pork chops, salt, pepper, cooking oil, flour, etc, etc. The list got longer and longer.

What do you have with pork chops? Hummm...., mashed potatoes and gravy, Okay add potatoes to the list. How about a veggie, English Peas! Okay add English peas to the list. Anyway, you get the idea, depending on how many days we would be gone, I would make a menu and then make a grocery list from the menu.

These trips usually lasted for three wonderful days and two glorious nights. The Coastal Resources captains and crew would usually ask, "How many wonderful days and glorious nights is this trip?" Those guys were sharp; they picked up on my sarcasm quickly. Sometimes, these trips would go on for five wonderful days and four glorious nights.

We would run to Redbird Creek dock near Richmond Hill the first day. The second day we would load fuel. If you've ever loaded fuel, you know the definition of "boring". Fuel trucks would arrive, I would climb on top of the trailer, check the "product", and see that it was the proper fuel and the tank was filled to the proper "load limit". I did that with every truck, you do not know how

Goin' Dialin'

embarrassing it is to deliver the wrong fuel to the wrong tank! I did it one time, never again.

Usually, the second day we would depart Redbird dock and head to Ossabaw. About a two-hour trip when loaded with fuel. We would arrive, hook up the diesel pump, and pump fuel for about five or six hours to the fuel tanks on the island. Gasoline was pumped into 1000-gallon tanks on trailers and hauled to the gasoline facility.

Third day, on a regular trip, we would depart Torrey Landing at Ossabaw and head for Sapelo. Or, go to Redbird Creek and pick up another load. Sometimes, we would have to take the barge to Savannah for gas-freeing and inspection. One trip in particular comes to mind....We were taking the barge to Savannah for gas freeing and inspection.

We left Ossabaw and got to Skidaway Marine Institute Dock and tied up for the night. We had the boat secured and I asked Freddie, "You want a beer?" Freddie said no, James G. was there helping us tie up, James was from our county. Freddie said that James," Would tell my wife about the beer!"

I stepped off the boat and shook James' hand," James, you want a beer?"

"No way! Freddie T's on that boat, he'll tell my wife!"

Goin' Dialin'

So, I spent the evening secreting beer to James and Freddie, what a pair!

Years went by.... where do the years go?! Teddy retired and Charles Durant sent George W along as the engineer. Anyone who knew George knows that George did everything fast!

Charles once said that George goes through life like he's killing a rattlesnake. So true!

George was like.....take a wild bird, put that bird in a cage and shake it continually, which was George on a barge trip. In the door George would go, open every cabinet, every drawer on the boat, and slam every one of them, out the door. "What the heck was that?" Freddie would ask.

"George." I would reply.

"Oh, yeah, George."

Wide open George. Hurry up and mess up George. Many names for him, all relate.

Then Charles sent Dan C...........''Should I check his pulse?" I'm not sure this guy's alive. Dan was soooo much the opposite of George.

We had just left Sapelo, Freddie makes an announcement to Dan and me, "That beer in the fridge is

Goin' Dialin'

for when we get tied up this evening, ya'll stay out of the beer until then."

Dan says, "OK Fred", pssshht, the beer can opens. I'm secretly trying to get Dan's attention, red Solo cup in hand, psst, Dan, pour me one in here!

Tug Boat Recipes

Pork Roast in the Crockpot

This is a killer, you cannot go wrong feeding a tug boat crew with this.
You will need:
Boston Butt
Potatoes
Carrots
Onions
Salt
Pepper

Directions: After leaving dock, sear the Boston butt in a skillet on all sides. Just turn a burner on wide open, and let the roast brown on each side.

Chunk it into the crock pot add a little water and turn it on low.

Take a break.

Cut up a couple of Vidalia onions, toss them into the crockpot.
Wash and cut up potatoes and carrots, throw them in.
Dowse this concoction with salt and pepper.

Let this simmer for 6 or 7 hours. I've never had a complaint about this, guys just scarf it down! It is so simple and sooo good!

Carolina Stew, Another one pot wonder (Low Country Boil)

You will need:
Shrimp
Sausage
Zatarains crab boil seasoning
Potatoes
Carrots
Corn on the cob
Rutabaga
Onions
Squash, or whatever else you want to throw in

Half fill the largest pot you have with water.
Bring it to a boil and add Zatarains seasoning bag.
Put in potatoes, onions, sausage, carrots and rutabagas.
When potatoes start getting soft, add corn and squash.
When potatoes get done, add shrimp.
Let this return to a boil and turn off heat.

Goin' Dialin'

Cover table with newspapers, drain liquid and dump the whole shebang onto the table.

Interviews

The late Harvey Hill was island manager on Sapelo for a few years. Harvey was a dynamo! A "get things done" kind of guy. We had tried to get new positions on the ferry for years, and we finally got two positions.

Harvey told me to prepare forty-six questions for the interview. Well I thought the request was odd, but I racked my brain and came up with as many real-life questions, things that we had gone through, situations that had actually happened. I squeezed my brain; I need a few more questions! Again, I thought the request was odd, why forty-six?

I approached Harvey a couple of days later with my questions. "I have thirty-eight; I just could not come up with forty six questions." Harvey looked at me like I had grown another head or something.

"I said, FOUR TO SIX!"

Dang, gotta get that hearing aid sometime soon!

Well, we both had a good laugh and then I got all serious. I had to make a confession to Harv.

Goin' Dialin'

"Harvey, I've never interviewed anyone before, and I have never actually been interviewed in my life."

Harvey was bewildered. "How do you work for the State of Georgia and never been interviewed?"

I explained that I was the only applicant for both jobs I'd had for the State, and the "interviews" were informal chats with both supervisors.

He said, "Well there's not much to it boy, we ask the questions, they answer them."

"What if they ask something that I don't know?" I asked.

"Just tell 'em, we're asking the questions here, not you!"

OK

I've been informed that they still, after 14 years of retirement, pull questions for interviews from my "wealth" of questions!

I do have some intuitive qualities, I told Harvey repeatedly that he should listen to me, I've been here awhile, and you can't get by with what you are doing! He wouldn't listen and soon, he was gone.

Goin' Dialin'

Fire on the Tugboat

We were headed to Nassau Bahamas with a dredge tow. The barge and the dredge equipment belonged to the dredge company. All we had to do was deliver it to the site. I was captain of the "William Breckinridge", which I renamed later to the "William Badluckinridge" or the "William Breakingthings." This was a 78-foot tug; we were towing a 200 foot barge astern. Well we got into "blue water", 1500 feet deep, the gulf stream. I went up to relieve my mate, Mark. He was concerned with a fuel filter and said that if I would shut the port engine off, he would change the filter before he went to bed. I think I said ok.

It was just about dark; Mark starts screaming, "FIRE, Fire in the engine room." That's not exactly what you want to hear when you are that far from land and there is 1500 feet of water below you. Talk about getting my attention!

Mark had loosened the fuel filter, which was for some really stupid reason was located over the exhaust of the engine. Diesel fuel hit the exhaust, and both being hot, ignited. We managed to get two fire extinguishers down to the engine room and put it out. I had an exit plan, barge ¼ mile behind us. Turn with the good engine, get everyone on the barge and cut the tow cable! We did manage to get the fire out and first aid to Mark, who suffered first degree burns, and we were happily back on our way to the Bahamas.

Things go south quickly in the ocean. There is a moment, a tipping of the scales, that is irreversible. You either live and learn or die.

I was telling my wife, Lucy, this story tonight. She said that I'd never told her this one. I said," Hum, guess I was hiding it from you so you wouldn't worry!"

I later almost sank the "William Breckinridge" in the Gulf of Mexico, but that's another story!

Bad Weather on the Sapelo Queen and the Annemarie

In my career as a boat captain, I have had some scary experiences. Lots of times the weather was perfect, and I had an awesome view out of my "office" window, sometimes it wasn't so perfect.

One thing that boat captains do very well is pass information, tips, a little knowledge that will keep the younger ones from looking bad, and maybe keep them alive. This is sort of built into the system, because to become a licensed boat captain, you must work under a licensed captain for a few years and learn from him/her.

Goin' Dialin'

The amount of time depends on the range and scope of the license you are seeking. I've had the good fortune of working with some terrific captains over the years.

My deckhand and I were trying to reach the ferry dock at Marsh Landing one afternoon on the Sapelo Queen during a severe thunderstorm. After being blown around and not being able to secure the bowline, I called him in and we backed away from the dock. Severe doesn't even come close to describing that weather! I don't know whether it was a microburst or a small tornado, but it was bad. When we backed away the wind caught me broadside and blew us about a quarter of a mile up the Duplin River.

Well, being young and dumb, I kept trying to "twin screw" the boat into the wind. Years later, and I've passed this information to every younger captain that I know, I learned that you cannot twin screw a boat in severe wind. Twin screwing is using your engines to turn the vessel. For example, if you want to pivot to the right, put your right engine in reverse gear, left engine in forward gear and turn the rudder to the right and in nice weather you pivot to the right and you look really good, like you know what you're doing! It is good when you look good because when your passengers and or crew lose confidence in you, well you are kind of ....unemployed.

I did finally turn that boat into the wind. Whew! After the worst of the storm passed, we got the boat tied up at Sapelo. The good thing about severe weather is that you,

Goin' Dialin'

well if you live through it, then have a story to share with other crazy boat captains.

Years later I was caught in a similar situation on the ferry "Annemarie". I've always told folks that I made two mistakes that day, the 8:30 am run and the 2:30 pm run. I let the McIntosh County Board of Education pressure me into running that day. It was tropical storm Earl (1998) which passed across the Florida panhandle and came our way. Schools were open; the pressure to run was on because transporting the island's school children was one of our mandates for the ferry operation. I should not have run that day. We tied up at Meridian dock after the 7:00 AM run and witnessed a tornado crossing through Meridian and into Doboy Sound. Not a real good sign, funnel clouds are never a good sign for smooth sailing.

Before we left Sapelo at 2:30 that afternoon, I had notified all commuters that we would run one trip and they should be ON IT! If they wanted to go home! We pulled away from the dock and the one thing that all the Sapelo ferries have in common is that they have a lot of "sail surface", meaning that they have large superstructures and shallow draft that allows wind to kind of "have its way" with them.

I had the commuters loaded on the boat, pulled away from Marsh Landing Dock, the wind caught me broadside at that moment and as I said, the ferries have a lot of sail surface. I kept trying to twin screw this boat into the wind, the results were dismal.

Goin' Dialin'

We were blown up the Duplin River. I finally gave up trying to "twin screw" the vessel around and put both engines in forward, cranked the rudder hard right and pushed both engines to their forward stops. Success! Just before we were going to be stuck in the marsh and I would have never, ever lived that one down! There may still be dents in the dash from me pushing the throttles so hard!

I've relayed that story to all younger captains that I know. First, if you do not feel comfortable running in the current weather, DON'T! You will get caught in severe weather sooner or later, I don't care how careful you are; don't try to twin screw into severe wind. Turn your rudder, full speed ahead is the only way you will break the winds hold.

But don't be a wimp either, run when you can!

Island Managers, Cars, Trucks and Trash

(Names are omitted to protect the stupid)

We went through many island managers during my twenty years running the ferry. All were good folks, some better than others and all had their own style of

Goin' Dialin'

management. Some were "hands off" when it came to the ferry operation others were sort of "meddlesome". I have been accused of making this story up, I swear to you it is true.

Not long after I moved to Sapelo, the island manager who hired me called me into his office to deliver some "FANTASTIC NEWS!"

We had a pickup truck at the mainland dock which we used to haul away trash, pickup U.S. Mail and run errands on the mainland. Everything was just lovely.

"I've got you a car!" He exclaimed, a bit too enthusiastically.

I had to think about that for a few moments, he was selling this idea to me a bit hard. I soon realized that it was his assigned car, a crappy little Ford Escort, that he had to unload on someone in order to get his new state truck. Dump it on the boat crew was always a popular option in such situations.

"Uh, I don't think that's gonna work." I replied. "We haul trash, it's nasty, it has garbage juices that leak out of the bags."

"We'll build you a trailer for the trash cans." Boy he's quick! "I'm concerned about ya'll hauling mail in the truck, what if it rains? The mail has to be protected."

"When it rains, we put it in the cab," I stated, "And, it has never been a problem." It's not like we have tons of

Goin' Dialin'

mail coming to Sapleo, usually there are only three bags about thirty percent full.

Well, we got the car, it was never an option. We waited on the trailer, never happened.

Six months later, in the middle of summer, Tracy and I had developed a routine for getting in the car. Open both doors, let the stench air out for a minute or two, hold your breath and start the car. Roll the windows down, all of them and hang you head out of the window while you drove to town.

After about a year of having the "stink mobile" we finally got another pickup truck, life was once again lovely. Then we got a new island manager, he was a reasonable guy, or so we thought.

He'd been our manager for about a year when he called me into his office for some REALLY GREAT NEWS!

"I'm concerned with the truck you have on the mainland, it has seen better days, I've decided to assign my car to the boat crew. I'm concerned with ya'll hauling the mail in that truck, it could get wet."

What did Yogi Berra say, Déjà vu all over again?

"We don't need a car, we had a car and it was ruined in a matter of months. We haul trash, it's nasty, the garbage juices leak on the carpet," of course my appeal was a waste of breath because he had a new truck coming and

Goin' Dialin'

he had to dump his Chevy station wagon off on somebody.

"We'll build you a trailer for the trash cans." Had he discussed this with the former island manager? This guy was famous for his practical jokes, I hoped this was one.

Well, about six months later, Tracy and I had the previous routine down pat. Open all four doors and the back hatch and let the stench out to the point you could get in, start it and roll all the windows down. Hang your head out of the window like a dog. No need to mention that the trailer never materialized.

After about a year we finally got another pickup truck. Life was once again lovely.

Five years and two island managers later, the island manager called me to his office for some REALLY GREAT NEWS! I was not excited.

"Got a car for the boat crew." He looked so happy. Happy to be getting rid of his huge Ford land barge so he could get his new truck.

I went into the complete saga of our mainland transportation history, the two state cars that probably went straight to the crusher after being ruined by us, and that WE DON'T WANT YOUR DAD-BLAMED CAR!

He surprised me by telling me that we could keep the truck for hauling garbage, but we were still getting the car. This guy was desperate to get his new truck.

Goin' Dialin'

"I want ya'll to have the car in case you have to pick up the commissioner or the governor from the airport." Wow! A new twist, I gave the guy an A for creativity.

I didn't mean to, but I started laughing, not discretely but belly laughing.

After regaining my composure, I asked," Do you think for one minute, that (names omitted, see above) would not run over me on the way to pick up the commissioner or the governor? I have never been asked to pick up VIP's from the airport."

He chuckled at my reply and said that I was right, but he had to get rid of his car. At least he was honest.

Sometime afterward, I read the "Seven Habits of Successful People" one of the habits is to be proactive.

The next island manager came along and while I was showing him around the boat operation, of which he wasn't familiar with in the least, I told him the epic story of the cars and trash.

"The boat crew does not want or need your car, if you are in line for a new vehicle, do not think that you can dump it off on us."

He agreed, but every once in a while, he would tell me that he had a car for us, just to get a rise out of me.

Goin' Dialin'

Island Managers and the pool

My brother Joe and I got "called to the carpet" on this and were asked nicely to refrain from getting up further pools on how long an island manager would last. By the Chief of Game Management, not a local supervisor!

As described in earlier stories, we went through quite a few island managers in our tenure on Sapelo Island. They usually only lasted for two years on average. They would then ascend the ladder of state government and move on.

Well, Joe and I had this ongoing pool of how long they would last. I usually went for one year and one day. That would cover me for the next entry which would be two years. We had this one nice young fellow, Joe asked me for my entry, one year, I said. I talked to the guy while I was barging his belongings over, called Joe and said," NO! Six months!"

Boy I was wrong; John was a fantastic island manager and has gone on to bigger and better things with the DNR.

Fire Truck

Many thanks for my sister-in-law for reminding me of this story. Joe and family were gone one weekend; he was the fire chief on Sapelo. Joe always knew what to do and what order to do it in when fighting fires; I on the other hand, am just a rookie.

We got a call that there was a woods fire on the north end of the island, this was somewhere around dark thirty. We rallied the fire department, loaded up the bulldozer with the fire plow and headed north. We unloaded the dozer, parked the eighteen-wheeler lowboy and started off with the bulldozer and fire plow very near the fire. The smoke was terrible, I flipped on the lights and all I could see were bushes! Bushes and smoke. I would turn the lights off, let my eyes adjust, and head toward the glow of the fire. I repeated this through the night.

Well, around one AM, we were stuck. Bulldozer stuck in the mud and fire close by. I asked Chris Bailey if he had ever chained a log to a dozer track and gotten out of a bog hole. He said he had heard of this method but never done it. I replied ditto. We found a log and got a chain off the lowboy, chained the log to the dozer track and got that sucker out of the bog hole! Whew!

We got the fire contained around three in the morning, all of us were whipped! I cut a firebreak around the eighteen-wheeler, cut a circle and parked the dozer in the middle. We looked over the terrain and parked the small fire truck in a place that had already burned, couldn't be safer!

Chris came beating on my front door later in the morning. "The fire truck burnt up!"

Goin' Dialin'

I knew he was kidding, we joke all the time. He swore up and down that he was not kidding. Off we drove to the north end.

Man, it looked like something from the Middle East! The truck was a burned-out hulk. The transmission housing was melted and looked like an aluminum pizza on the ground under it. Not a good endorsement for our fire department. I remember thinking that I'll never live this one down. Joe leaves me in charge for one weekend and I manage to burn up the fire truck!

Joe and I went and toured the scene when he returned on Sunday. I explained the weird fire break that had crazy loops. I was on the bulldozer, in the dark, when I turned on the lights all that I could see was bushes, totally lost in the woods. I ordered and attached a compass to the bulldozer and Joe had a good laugh over that. Hey, I was a boat captain for 25 years, give me a compass and I'm okay, leave me with lights, bulldozer and woods, I'm lost!

Several years later, we were reforming our little fire department, they elected me chief.

Go figure.

Goin' Dialin'

Almost Sank!

When I was tug boating, we had a project in the Gulf of Mexico where I had to work for a few weeks. We were "re-nourishing" the beach at Clearwater Florida. This meant that we were hired by the dredge company to pump sand from the harbor at Tampa, haul it to Clearwater and pump it to the beach. I never liked "construction" projects, I like to make tow to a barge and go somewhere! New York, Connecticut, Rhode Island, construction projects to me were boring. Same place for weeks on end.

We had been standing by, for several days, inshore at Clearwater. I told the dredge captain that we had severe weather coming in the next day. That next morning, they called us to assist with getting the offshore equipment and bringing it inshore. Picked a fine time to do that!

We went out of the harbor, into rough seas and started bringing the dredge equipment inshore. We tied off to a barge and started towing it in. Well, something slowed us, and I put more power to the tug and got headed in. First mistake, if something slows you in the ocean, it may mean something is wrong! The boat wasn't feeling right, kind of heavy feeling, I told the deckhand to go check the engine room, wake up the off-duty deckhand and don lifejackets.

He came back up in a panic," We're goin' down Capn'!!! We're taking on water!!" I told him to start the

Goin' Dialin'

bilge pumps, and crank up the two-inch gasoline powered pump, but put the suction low, and avoid pumping any oil from the engine room. I got on the radio, handed the barge off to another tug and started heading in. We had so much support from the dredge company, they brought more gasoline powered pumps and we managed to get inshore.

That was the closest thing to sinking a boat that I've ever encountered, all the training kicks in. The funniest thing was the poor off duty deckhand who woke up to the emergency, thought the other deckhand was fooling with him until he saw a hotdog rolling across the galley floor. Later he told me that he knew it was serious when he got to the wheelhouse and I had my lifejacket zipped and fastened. I always wore it loose!

Later, we would discover that we had seven slices across the bottom of the tug. We temporarily sealed them with wooden wedges.

When all goes wrong offshore, and it can really fast, as I mentioned earlier there is a tipping point. A point of no return when you either live or die. I found out later that the steel spuds that hold the dredge in place had been broken off. I managed to run over one of those spuds.

That night, when I was finally going to the shower, I kicked off my clothes and threw them in the trash. We had worked most of the day staying afloat. The water had flooded the pans that catch engine oil and there was a layer of oil all over the engine room which we soaked up in our clothes while plugging the holes.

When the Coast Guard investigator called to interview me, he asked if there was anything that would have prevented this incident. I said," Well, yeah, if someone had told me there was a broken off spud right there....it would have helped tremendously! He agreed.

One point, we did not pump any oil overboard during this crisis, we were aware, kept the suction intakes low and did not get any fines. So even in a crisis, training kicks in and saves the boat and the environment!

Lost Tourists

I was minding my own business one afternoon, this was during the time Ike and I were living at the Marsh Landing House on Sapelo, when someone knocked on my door.

I greeted a stranger at the door, who had a map in one hand, and he immediately asked, "I've read about the nature trails on Blackbeard Island and was looking for where they start."

"On Blackbeard," I replied.

"This is Blackbeard," *he was convinced.*

Goin' Dialin'

"No, this is Sapelo,"

He proceeded to show me my error on his map. The Duplin River was actually Blackbeard Creek, he knew exactly where he was.

After arguing for a couple of minutes, I finally convinced him that I was right, he was wrong. He left and I'm sure everyone has this moment of thinking of the perfect comeback about two minutes too late. When he was out of sight, it came to me. I should have said to him, "Dang lying real estate agent!"

Our ferry route took us across the Intracoastal Waterway (ICW) at Doboy Sound, boats approaching the sound would start following us. Some would pass us when we were headed to the mainland, stop when they got to the end of the sound where Atwood Creek, Manchester Cut go north and Hudson creek, Carnigan River go south. They always ignored my calls on the VHF radio, because they just knew I was going to complain about their wake on the passing. After they realized their dilemma and stopped, they would call me. Aha! That radio works after all! My friend and co-worker, Frank Price always disdainfully called a person like this, "A doctor in a Sea Ray."

I remember one guy from South Carolina following me all the way to Marsh Landing Dock on Sapelo. He was confused and totally lost. "Get out your chart and I'll show you where you are," I said.

Goin' Dialin'

"Chart?"

"Map," I replied.

He pulled out a road map, I kid you not.

The availability of GPS chart plotters has greatly reduced the number of "followers" these days.

Mike and Ike

When Ike turned 12 years old, I decided it was time for him to have his own truck. I got with a scientist on Sapelo named Alice Chalmers (yep, that's also the name of a tractor), she oversaw liquidating the assets of a scientist who had recently moved from Sapelo; he had this really great 1970 (Ike corrected me on this, it was a 1972) Chevrolet truck. Ike and I wanted it; we met Alice at the "hanger". R.J. Reynolds was really into aviation and built a 5000-foot grass airstrip on Sapelo and a really nice hanger. Hey, they used to land DC-3's there, I think.

OK, you may be asking, "12 years old and you thought it was time to have his own truck?" Hey, it's Sapelo Island, there are no restrictions on underage drivers, I've taught many 12-year old's to drive. He's 38 now so the statute of limitations has certainly expired, if you want to call DFACS.

Goin' Dialin'

Well, until he was 13, I only let him drive while I was in the truck with him. Then I only let him drive to his Uncle Joe's, about two miles from our house at Marsh Landing. (Eat your hearts out soccer moms. They are all thinking, dang, I have to shuttle the children everywhere!) I did require him to call me when he got there and when he left. Of course, that rarely happened.
This truck had a three-speed transmission on the steering column, commonly known in early years as "three on the tree." The shift collar wore out one day and Ike and I were discussing what we should do to fix it. I came up with the brilliant idea that we should stick a lever through the floorboard, use it to shift reverse and first gear, and the column to shift second and third gears. I found a piece of 1/2" metal conduit in our storage shed, drilled a hole in it, but the extension cord wasn't long enough to reach the truck. I took a hammer and chisel to cut a slot in the floorboard. A 1970 Chevy truck is built with a little more steel than is common today! I said to Ike," Hand me that .22 rifle, and stand back." This was before the days of cordless drills.

"POW", hole in floor! I took the chisel and made a slot for the conduit, we had that truck going in no time! It did take a little getting used to. Shift to first on the floor, press the clutch, knock the floor shifter to neutral, go to column shift and shift to second and third. Worked like a charm! .22 rifle, the original cordless drill!

Flare Gun

Fred Hay reminded me of this story several years ago, I heard it from his brother, Andy, last weekend, we had a 30th anniversary of Mike and Ike on Sapelo, we moved there on April 1, 1985. I always call it Sapelo's greatest April fool's joke. (It is now 33 years, without fatalities I might add)

Fred was pregnant, correction, Rene' was in the family way with Katie. Someone told Fred that he now had to be responsible; he was going to be a father. His reply, " Let me tell you about Mike and Ike." Fred drove up into the yard one day. Ike and I were hiding behind the corner of the house at Marsh Landing, where we lived for 19 years. We were conducting an experiment. I had purchased many of those flare gun kits for boats. They say 12-gauge on the barrel. Plastic barrel. Well, I mean dang, you just have to think, "Will a 12-gauge shotgun shell shoot in this plastic gun?"
OK, experiment: Will a 12-gauge shotgun shell shoot in a 12-gauge, plastic, flare gun? We duct taped the flare gun to a fence post in the backyard, ran fishing line to the trigger, loaded the flare gun with a 12-gauge bird shot shell. We hid around the corner of the house to pull the trigger, and Fred shows up. Dang, a witness! Well, we had to explain the whole thing to Fred, whose curiosity got the best of him and he was in.

The results of the flare gun test were; yes, a flare gun will fire a 12-gauge shotgun shell, once. It split the barrel, would probably be safe for one firing if you absolutely had to do it, but not recommended.

The Truck Chain Method

Ike named this, "the truck chain method", and since its inception we've used it many times with varying success. The first time was when we had trouble removing a lower unit from an outboard motor. This was Ike's idea, chain the motor to a tree, back the pickup truck up to the lower unit and chain it to the truck, pull hard. I'd watched the UGA mechanic, Teddy, cut holes in the exhaust housing and insert a torch to heat the drive shaft and crankshaft. All that looked like waaay too much work and damaged the outboard. Ike's idea sounded pretty good to me. Anyway, we plopped the 120 HP Johnson on the ground, chained it up appropriately, and gave it a pull. Nothing. Okay, backed up and snatched it real good and bingo! Success! From that time on, when we had a dilemma such as bent bumpers, dents, whatever, Ike would suggest "the truck chain method". And it usually worked.

Weighing a shark

The things we do on Sapelo Island. Most out of necessity, some just because it's fun. Ike called me from shark fishing in the boat one evening, had a five-

Goin' Dialin'

foot shark under tow (I've been corrected! This shark was closer to eight feet). A five-footer is too heavy to load in the boat by himself, so he would just tie a rope to it and tow it in. I don't even remember how many times he did this, he would call, I would round up help and we'd meet him at the dock and pull the shark onto the floating dock, up the ramp and into the truck. There was always the promise of an upcoming shark fry, so help was usually easy to find.

I do remember this particular shark because we decided to weigh it. Dr. Lloyd had a 200 lb scale at the Botany trailer and for some insane reason he had left a key to the trailer with Ike, Lloyd was back at Georgia Tech at that time. He was teaching one day a week, I think it was on Wednesday, and he complained constantly about that. I said, " Lloyd, you have to work one day a week, is the pay the same?" "Well, yeah." "Well duh! For a PhD, you sure are a dimwit." Ike went and got the scale, but then we had the dilemma of how we were going to get the shark hanging under it. One of us had the brilliant idea of attaching the scale to a rope and another rope between the shark and the scale and pulling it over a live oak limb with a pickup truck.

Well, all went well until the shark left the ground! Springs and all sorts of stuff exploded from the 200 lb. scale! So, how much does a five-foot shark weigh? Well, obviously over 200 pounds. We found out later that it's closer to 300 pounds. But, we caught grief from Dr. Dunn for years about ruining his scale! He kept the

Goin' Dialin'

remains on display at the Botany Trailer for quite some time, as a matter of fact, I'm sure he still has it!

Drum Launch

This is more than likely totally illegal. It's been at least 15 years so maybe the statute of limitations is in my favor. Our friend, Dr. Lloyd, wanted to blast some stumps off his lot. I told him that the easiest way is with ammonium nitrate and diesel fuel, I did this several times with Jim Evans. We used prima cord to send the shock wave needed to ignite the ammonium nitrate. Jim and I did this to blast water holes for wildlife during droughts. Ike and I didn't have access to prima cord, as it is a controlled substance, and no one in his or her right mind was going to give Ike and me access to such. We had to come up with another solution. After talking it over with James M., we decided that acetylene and oxygen would do the trick. Dr. Lloyd of the famous "Botany trailer" where you could find anything you needed, supplied the "trigger", resistor wire.
We had a 55-gallon drum, left over from the stability test on the Sapelo Queen; this drum had no top, so we flipped it over and buried the open end in the dirt. We ran a hose into the drum, added acetylene and oxygen through the hose. We connected the trigger to a 12-volt car battery and KABOOM! Thinking that we were going to have a really good explosion, we were surprised when the 55-gallon drum LAUNCHED! That sumbadagun went; I do not exaggerate, an estimated 400

feet in the air! Then we watched as it fell back to earth, "Oh, Crap!" Here it comes! Yikes! It landed a few feet away from where it launched, but it was tense there for a few seconds, which seemed like hours! And the Mike and Ike Confederate Space Program was born.

How to go hunting with the game warden

Several years ago, the statute of limitations has passed; Mike H. and I had finished a barge trip to Ossabaw Island and returned to Sapelo. Mike was a wildlife technician with law enforcement certification. It was early afternoon and I asked Mike if he wanted to shoot some doves at Bush Camp. He said he had no shotgun on the island. Well Ike and I had several, so I told him I would loan him one, and shells, no problem. He said, "Great, let's do it."
We shot a few doves that afternoon and when we finished up I asked Mike why he didn't even ask if I had a hunting license, him being a game warden. He said that he figured that I had a license; I mean I'm hunting with the game warden! How dumb can you be? I told him I didn't have a hunting license and asked if he was going to write me up. Before he could answer I informed him that he would have to write himself up as well.
He asked why. I said that I may be hunting without a license, but you are hunting with an unplugged shotgun!
And that my friend is how you hunt with the game warden.

Goin' Dialin'

Alford

Alford and I worked together for 20 years, he was my friend, my pal, my co-worker and my go to man. (Hey, I saved his life once!) When I went to the funeral home to see Walfie (that was what I always called him) for the last time, I got all choked up and sat on a pew. Nathan, the funeral director, came over, put his hand on my shoulder and said," I know how you feel, he was your right-hand man." Nathan, Alford and I had loaded many caskets on the ferry. Folks that I dearly loved, Viola Johnson, Benny Johnson, Viola Bailey, Cracker Johnson, Fred Johnson, Earl Walker(my best friend), Allen Greene, Annie Mae Green, Willie Greene, Nancy Greene and many others. I gave many Sapelo residents their last ride to the Island.

I told Nathan that Walfie was my right-hand man, my left-hand man and my in the middle man, a good man Walfie was. We used to have a ritual for anyone who worked on the ferry, we would stop in Doboy sound, shut off the engines and generator, and have one minute of silence, and drift. I hope the crew is still observing this. This is a good sendoff for a boatman.

I asked Alford if he wanted to eat lunch at B and J's one day and he accepted the offer.

Goin' Dialin'

When we got there, the rude waitress was working, this was many years ago. This waitress would throw the menus on the table and ask, "Watta ya want!" It was a game and we always tried to be as rude as possible to each other.

I asked, "Where's the good-looking waitress today?"
Alford like to have hurt himself laughing! Well, after our glasses ran out of iced tea, we decided not to use that line with any waitress ever again!

After that, Alford used to warn people, "Don't go to lunch with Mike, he ain't goin' to win no academy award, cause he don't know how to act. I like to have thirsted to death at lunch with Mike and forget the to-go cups."

Took me a long time to get Alford to eat with me again! I had to promise to be nice.

Deer hunting

Alford told me this story once, a long time after it happened.
Now mind you, this is Sapelo Island. The folks here have always been self-sufficient. When you ran out of venison you went and harvested another deer, as simple as that. Alford's uncle, Allen Green was a wonderful man, I once took pictures of him making his baskets, he was a great artisan and human being. He told me several

times that he," didn't like white people, he loved white people. I love everybody." That was Allen's anthem.
Now when you read the rest of this story, please don't go calling PETA or anyone else. Please don't send me any nasty letters or posts, this is just how things are on Sapelo.
Alford's Uncle Allen Greene told him to go out and get a deer; they were running out of venison. Of course, everyone knows that the best time to get a deer is at night. Alford walked a short way from the house and spotted deer eyes in his light. He shot right between the eyes with his .22 rifle. Dead deer. OK, closer inspection, Dead Dog! Alford had shot his own dog, he was sick over that!

Coffee

Anyone remember the Sapelo Queen? I bought a coffee maker for the Sapelo Queen one winter. I usually made coffee before the 7 am run, or when we got to the mainland at 7:30.
One morning Alford said he would make the coffee. He did and when it was ready I poured myself a big mug full. I took one sip and exclaimed, "Dang! Walfie, how much coffee did you put in here?" He said he filled the filter up. I asked if he measured it. "No, just filled the filter holder up." I said, "You're supposed to measure it, one teaspoon per cup."
"Measure it?" was his reply

Goin' Dialin'

Lawn Mower

When I moved to Sapelo to run the ferry in 1985, we had a push lawnmower. This was a Briggs and Stratton 3.5 HP mower that the crew used to cut the grass at both docks. Every couple of weeks they would put it on the ferry and cut the little bit of grass at Meridian. This was back before the parking lot at Marsh Landing on Sapelo was paved and we had grass to cut. I took the mower in for repairs and maintenance a couple of times over the years. The mower was finally done for, it was over 20 years old, parts weren't available, etc. Well, Fred M. was managing the SINERR at the time and had bought a couple of push lawnmowers from Tait's in Brunswick. (Trey Tait happens to be a first cousin of mine).

I asked Fred if we could have one of the lawnmowers assigned to the ferry. His answer was no. "Ya'll will just tear it up". I told Fred that I begged to differ with him, we've had this lawnmower for over 20 years, it's worn out, no parts available, etc. This exchange went on for a couple of weeks and Fred finally relented and gave us one of the new push mowers.

Well, by that time the grass was fairly tall. Alford fired the brand-new lawnmower up and mowed six feet, I measured it, six feet. He ran over a screw jack that someone had left there in the grass. Bent the crankshaft on the new mower!

I took it back to Trey, "Can you fix it?"

Trey said it was cheaper to buy a new mower. I explained that in the government's way of doing things, I had no "equipment" money, but I had lots of "repairs" money. I said," Cuz, just fix it! Please."

In the meantime, Fred asked me why the grass wasn't cut when he had given us a brand-new lawn mower. I told him that we had to take it to Tait's for a little warranty work, it just wasn't running right. The six-foot swath just screamed," Liar, liar."

We finally got the mower back and Alford cut the grass, after both of us searched the remaining area for more "surprises".

Doctor on the Cell Phone

I still hurt myself laughing when I think of this story!
Alford and I were working on the Annemarie, making the regular 8:30 am run one morning in the early '90's. Cell phones were just coming out and they were bag phones. We had our first one on the Annemarie, we specified that it come with a cell phone.

This Doctor who was on the tour asked if he could plug his bag phone into our 12-volt outlet, he had some emergency to tend to. I told him sure, I'm running along in Doboy Sound and the Annemarie wasn't the fastest boat in the world, and I'm bored anyway. The doc plugged in and called someone named Shirley, his office manager I presume. He kept yelling into the phone, "Shirley, I can barely hear you Shirley!" Repeatedly. And I mean repeatedly.

Goin' Dialin'

Alford did his famous chuckle, leaned over and whispered to me, "He's got the phone backwards." I looked over and sure enough, he was trying to talk through the wrong side of the handset. Then Alford left, I looked back at the rear deck and he is doubled over laughing!

Meanwhile, I'm trying to keep a straight face and not let the doctor see that I'm laughing at him. Bad for public servants to laugh at the people we serve!

Alford clued me in on what was going on, then left! I had to wait until we got to Sapelo and unloaded before I could double over laughing. I kept telling him," You ain't right!" and we laughed and laughed.

The bag phones of the early 90's were exactly opposite of the land line phones of the time, the key pad was on the back of the bag phone, that's why it was easy for the doctor to mistakenly hold it backwards.

I made a note of the doctor's name, and made a point of never seeing him for any reason.
Call me quirky.

Goin' Dialin'

Saved his life

Alright might not have actually saved his life, but I kept him from a public butt whoppin! We were at the Trough, the bar on Sapelo, this was way back in the late 80's.(This is when we were young and dumb!) There was a group of college girls there, drinking and dancing, we were having a good time! This was the night that Findley Anderson did his great "John Travolta" move, whipped off his jacket and bingo, lassoed the light fixture and ripped it out of the ceiling.

I don't know about you, but when I'm in a bar, and I hear glass break, well, I'm kinda out of there! I figure that there ain't nothing good happening here!

Things settled down, the glass was cleaned up. I went to the bathroom, which was a one holer and was busy at the time. I did what all us Sapelonians do and went outside. I was taking care of business and as I looked down the road, I saw Alford's wife, Mary, coming down the road toward the Trough.

I went in and found Alford, he was on the dance floor with the college girls.

"Walfie, Mary is coming!"

"Whut?" he replied

"Man, I saw Mary walking this way; get your butt off the dance floor!"

He did, she arrived, and everything was cool.

Sardine Scam

Alford taught me a valuable lesson one day without even trying. He had a can of sardines; it was the last run of the day back to Sapelo. He was signing up all the widow women; there was Ruth Wilson, Ruth Johnson and Viola Johnson. He pulled this dilapidated can of sardines out of his pocket and asked if any of them would like to share his "dinner". Needless to say, the ladies were appalled. He got three; count 'em, three, invitations to dinner that night! And I mean GOOD dinners! After viewing this, I dubbed it the sardine scam. OK, I tried it, except with Spam, worked like a charm!

I asked Alford how long he had that can of sardines; you could hardly read the label. "Heh, heh, heh, a long time."

Vienna Sausages

I caught the 3:30 boat on a Thursday when I was off one day. I went upstairs to the wheel house of the Sapelo Queen as usual. Alford and Tracy had been rebuilding the wooden grate that was on the back deck of the Queen that day. Apparently, they didn't have time to stop for lunch. Tracy had gone down to the little store at Meridian to get lunch for both of them. He got one can of Vienna Sausages and one sleeve of saltine crackers.

Goin' Dialin'

Now all you gourmet chefs know, there are seven of those wonderful sausages per can. Tracy explained to Alford that he was the oldest, so he got four of the seven Vienna Sausages; crackers apparently weren't divided by age or otherwise. Alford was scarfing down a Vienna Sausage and a cracker, I said," That looks good Walfie, can I have one?" He said," Help yourself." I just laughed and said," I wouldn't dream of it!" Alford laughed and from that day, if I asked him how many sausages were in a can, or if the oldest gets the most, etc., we would have a great laugh!

My good friend and co-worker, Jake responded to my offer of Vienna Sausages when we were fishing one day. He said the first sausage is the best thing you ever tasted and the last is the worst! I've found Jake's words to be true. The other grey meat.

Alford's complaint

I was sitting in my office one morning. Alford came in after the first ferry run and announced," I have a complaint." Mind you, I've been working with Walfie for nearly twenty years, he had never said those words to me before. I was stunned. I told him to pull up a chair, have a seat, I want to hear this! This is going to be good!

I don't even remember what his complaint was, I know that I handled it and Walfie was happy. But the fact that he had a complaint after 20 years of working together just floored me. He never complained!

Tommy

Bless the dead, as they say on Sapelo, anytime you talk about someone who has passed away, you start with their name and add, "Bless the dead."

Tommy was a trip, I loved him, and I hated him, was ready to kill him at one point.

Lucy came across a 1/3-acre lot on Sapelo back in 1995. She bought it sight unseen because it was the only property for sale on Sapelo at the time. She was sitting in the school superintendent's office, ready to interview her for the local newspaper. When the superintendent got off the phone, she said, "Sorry, my brother wants to sell his lot on Sapelo."

Lucy said," Call him back! Tell him it's sold!!!"

Sight unseen, it took two trips from the surveyor to locate this lot. We thought for a while that it was under water! Glasco (Bless the dead) located it, it was high and dry. (Remember, I'd much rather be lucky than good!)

Goin' Dialin'

I'd always wanted to build a house, thought that would be the ultimate guy accomplishment. Well, building one on a remote island turned out to be that. I told Lucy once that I was going to build a picnic table one weekend so that I could remember what a project is. This house was two years in the making! Project just doesn't seem to describe it!

We poured 20 tons of concrete in the footing, 500 bags of Kwikrete, and some Portland cement added to get the psi needed to meet the engineer's specs. We went with Insteel, a product that was then produced in Brunswick, GA.

We got the insteel panels up, they were cut to our specifications, and a thunderstorm came up and blew the whole thing down, Dang, start over. Did it again. Got crazy Nick there to spray concrete on the whole thing. Nick was great on that part, but had a drug problem and kinda spazzed out on the finish coat.

We subbed out several jobs to Tommy and Joe W., a pair if there ever was one. Tommy was a good builder but would take shortcuts whenever he could get away with it. Tommy had a speech impediment and would pronounce words wrong. "Bolt" became "boat", "tar paper" became "tile paper", "platform" became "pratform".

When we got to the roof, it is a steep roof and I decided to sub that part to Tommy and Joe since I wanted no part of that job.

Goin' Dialin'

Tommy had this "great idea" to attach one piece of decking at a time and shingle each as he went.

"One problem," I said, "You can't get continuous runs of felt under the shingles that way."

"Don't need no tile paper." Tommy responded.

I just stared at him, speechless. When I finally regained my composure, he and I argued about it the rest of the afternoon.

The next morning, before I left to pick them up. I told Lucy, "If Tommy mentions 'tile paper' this morning, I'm going to take a two by four and beat him to death!"

I picked up Tommy and Joe and he never mentioned his stupid shortcut again.

Gnats, You've Got to Hate 'Em, You've Got to Love 'Em

Coastal Georgia sand gnats are nasty little creatures. They like to swarm, they like to bite. They bite like democrats vote, early and often, and after you smash them they keep on making you itch after they are dead. Lovely creatures.

Goin' Dialin'

If you travel inland from the Georgia coast you will meet up with bigger gnats that don't bite. They just constantly fly in your face, get in your eyes, ears and mouth and are just annoying. We do get them occasionally on the coast, they are particularly bad after a forest fire.

Stanfield, my buddy on Ossabaw, always called them, "Dog ass knockers"

I asked him why and he told me that normally, "They've usually been knocking around a dog's ass right before they fly into your face." Yuck.

Back to our biting and really irritating gnats on the coast. When I was running the Sapelo Queen back in the eighties and early nineties, I found that if I positioned myself on the eastern railing, the usual afternoon ocean breeze, which is from the southeast, hit the superstructure of the boat, ran down the side and gave me a nice cool gnat free station in which to greet tourists. The tourists did not figure that out. They would come down carrying luggage, drop it, start swatting gnats and ask me if the gnats were always this bad.

Oh, I love this part, my response was always, I had two:

"What gnats?"

Or, "No, they are usually much worse!"

Heh, heh, heh.

Goin' Dialin'

Okay, there are two reasons why I stated above that we "love gnats." One, according to my friend and retired professor, Lloyd, shrimp eat the eggs or larva or something that is the beginning of the gnat life cycle. (Remember Lloyd is a scientist, I just don't pay much attention to what he says, so I don't remember exactly the facts of the matter.) I do like shrimp, as Bubba in the movie Forest Gump said, "Fried shrimp, boiled shrimp, baked shrimp, broiled shrimp, shrimp and potatoes, shrimp and onions, shrimp and grits, etc." I've never met a shrimp I didn't like in one of those recipes. I do have some dynamite recipes to share with you later, don't worry, they're coming. So, we need to put up with the gnats to have the shrimp.

The other reason, which comes from yours truly, is that if it weren't for sand gnats and the dark water we have on the Georgia coast, we would be up to our asses in Yankees! So, you must love them for that little gift.

Recipes

I promised to include these fabulous recipes that I have enjoyed! I couldn't decide whether to include them in one section or spread them out through the book. Hey, it's my book! I can put them wherever I please!

I may have to split this into serious recipes and guy recipes. On second thought, if you bought my book, you are obviously an intelligent person and can figure out which recipes are serious, and which are "guy recipes".

Charles and Lloyd's delicious Charleston Redfish

This is really good because, back me up on this guys, you start with a stick of butter. Man, if you start with a stick of butter, how can you possibly go wrong?

Take your honey redfish fishing.

Catch redfish. (If redfish are not 14 inches long, have a spare tire in the back of your truck, drop undersized redfish in the center ring of the spare tire, the game wardens never looks there. Of course, they might now, since I let that little secret out.)

Fillet redfish.

Preheat oven to 350 degrees (Fahrenheit, none of these are in that goofy Celsius stuff)

Chunk a cast iron skillet in the oven.

Oh yeah, start a pot of rice. If you don't know how to cook a pot of rice, you may need a wife, as you are hopeless. Follow instructions on rice bag, it works guys!

When the cast iron skillet gets hot, and I mean forevermore hot, toss in the stick of butter.

When that butter starts to brown, ohh, that's when it gets good, put redfish fillets in the skillet.

When the redfish gets about done, pour in 1 cup of white wine.

Serve redfish and the liquid butter and wine on top of the rice. Your woman will think you are a genius!!!!

Fish and Grits

Sharing this is personal for me because this is how I won Lucy's heart.

Step 1: Take your honey fishing.

Step 2: Catch some trout. (If trout are not 13 inches long, use spare tire method above to get them home)

Step 3: Fillet trout.

Step 4: Put on a pot of grits. (Again, if you must ask how to do this, you really need a wife or a basic cooking course. You can follow the directions on the bag of grits, after you dig it out of the trash.)

Step 5: Fry trout. Mix one-part flour and one-part corn meal for batter. (See step 4 above)

Step 6: Be prepared for the woman you are serving to fall madly in love with you!

The best story of fish and grits....

When I serve fish and grits, I must tell this story.

Bill B. was suing the State of Georgia for not allowing him access to his legally purchased property on Sapelo Island. His lawyer, the late Dan White of Darien (Bless the dead) made a point of wearing a simple suit to the trial. He looked over at the state lawyers, I think there were three of them in three-piece suits, and stated," These people think they can come down from Atlanta, in their three-piece suits and take our property, just 'cause we eat fish and grits for breakfast." That was the best dang argument from a lawyer ever. He won the case.

Spam

I asked my step-granddaughters, Lucy and Taylor if they wanted a Spam and cheese omelet one morning while they were visiting.

"What is Spam?", Lucy asked.

Goin' Dialin'

I replied that Spam is an acronym for Super Precious Awesome Meat.

They declined.

Lucy later informed me that she had been to the "store" on Sapelo, found a can of Spam and read the ingredients, I told her that was a "no, no". You never want to know what exactly is in Spam. She was determined to let me know the ingredients. Some sort of meat, don't know where it came from, and meat by products, of unknown origin. You just don't need to know these details!

Spam and Cheese Omelet

2 eggs
Spam
Cheese

Dice Spam into little cubes
Break eggs
Stir eggs
Heat skillet

Dump eggs into skillet
Add spam and cheese
Fold
Enjoy!!

Goin' Dialin'

International Gut Buster

One of my favorite sandwiches! You will need:
1 can of Vienna Sausages
1 Vidalia Onion
1 Slice of Swiss Cheese
Mayo
Bread

Carefully open the Vienna Sausages, don't bruise those little morsels while you remove them from the can. Slice sausages lengthwise. Since there are seven of these wonderful creations in a can, you will now have fourteen pieces.
Snack on a couple of the sausages while you create this gourmet meal, you have plenty. Spread lots of mayonnaise on your bread. Lay those lovely sausage halves on the bread. Cut a thick slice of Vidalia (pronounced Vi-day-yuh) onion and carefully place on the sausages. Add a slice of Swiss cheese on top.

There are two ways to accomplish this next part. You can pretreat your stomach with an acid reducer or crumble a couple of Rolaids on top of the cheese. Either way, it is a palatable wonderland just waiting for you between two slices of bread!

Tamale and Chili Casserole

Goin' Dialin'

I found this recipe on the back of a can of tamales, it's a keeper.
You will need:
One can tamales
One can of chili
Cheese

Open a can of tamales
Open a can of chili
Grate some cheese

Put the tamales on the bottom of a casserole dish, should I mention that you need to remove the corn husks from the tamales? Maybe. Dump in some of the grated cheese. Douse this with the can of chili. Add more cheese on top.

Bake at 350 degrees until cheese on top is bubbly and a little brown. This should be about twenty minutes.

Delish!

Spamgetti

You will need:

1 can of Spam
Spaghetti noodles
Spaghetti sauce

Goin' Dialin'

Boil spaghetti noodles until done, if done, when you throw one at the wall, it will stick.
Open Spam, carefully remove this delicacy from the can, chop it up.
Open jar of Ragu, or other brand of spaghetti sauce.
Sauté Spam in a pan, when it browns, add Ragu (Using the dos X guy's voice) I don't cook very often, but when I do…it's with Ragu. Serve, be prepared for a delight to your taste buds!

I hope you have enjoyed my little book. I certainly enjoyed writing all those stories down. It just always amazes me how little things, small details can change your entire life.

Goin' Dialin'

If my sister-in-law's uncle had not been a TV repairman for Sears, all of this would never have happened. He traveled to Sapelo Island sometime around 1975 to repair a television for one of the DNR employees. He got to talking to the customer and found out that there was a mechanic's job opening soon on the island. My brother, Joe applied and got the job.

If Jim Whitted and I had not been on that boat in 1992, and I had not confiscated the beer from Lucy.

Where would we be?

Fact is stranger than fiction.

Made in the USA
Columbia, SC
30 May 2021